T0195563

LOS MILEROS

The 1,000 pound cotton pickers during the 1940s-60s in America.

MARTINIANO CHAPA JR.

authorHOUSE

AuthorHouse™
1663 Liberty Drive
Bloomington, IN 47403
www.authorhouse.com
Phone: 833-262-8899

Published by AuthorHouse 01/11/2024

ISBN: 978-1-7283-0607-0 (sc)
ISBN: 978-1-7283-0606-3 (hc)
ISBN: 978-1-7283-0605-6 (e)

Library of Congress Control Number: 2019942716

Print information available on the last page.

This book is printed on acid-free paper.

This book is dedicated to my family and all those who have suffered the pain of leaving their homes to go out picking cotton in the fields in order to make a living supporting their families. Their sacrifice is remembered and appreciated.
I honor them!

Martíniano Chapa Jr.

CONTENTS

Cover Design:
Nick Danzi - Front Cover Illustration
Laura Herrera- Back Cover Design

INTRODUCTION

Tears of My Past, Tears of Jubilation

Why you are crying, old man?

Well, for a moment, I was thinking I was back in the day when I was a milero. My tears are of joy for what was then, working so hard in the cotton fields. The world of the cotton picker was not a walk through the park or a vacation. It was very demanding and brutal work. We found ways to overcome it knowing that with positive thinking and hard work, we could reach the place of the mileros.

The tears are remembering those days back then. I was young but high strung and always trying to pick a thousand pounds of cotton in one day. When I did, that was my greatest accomplishment in the cotton fields, a labor of love.

These are also tears of sadness for the days growing up in the cotton fields. These tears are of missing those days, which bought happiness to my family, especially my parents. So every time I go back to the past, my parents are there; they are no longer on this earth, but when I go into the past, they are there, and will always be.

Were we crazy back then? No, we were not, but we were a proud family working as hard as we could to make a living. For the stronger cotton pickers, there was always a desire to reach that milestone, that far-away marker, that invincible goal, the one-thousand-pound barrier ~ to become a milero. Getting there brought a feeling of pride, a joyful feeling that you had achieved greatness for that day and had accomplished something very special, something remarkable. The adrenaline you felt as you were getting closer to your goal was extreme, irresistible, and compelling. Sometimes, it was you and your mind talking to each other, your mind trying to convince your body that you were not exhausted, that you were too proud to stop.

What a past we had to live through; it was madness. Well, that madness put food on our table, and it gave us a chance for a better life. It gave us way to survive, hope, and a steppingstone to a better future. That's why this old man is crying these tears of memories about my youth and my teen years spent in the cotton fields. They were extraordinary years, and the tears are of joy. What more could I ask? There is not any anguish in me but happiness, so do not worry about this old man crying.

Especially when he goes back to the day to embrace his past and his loving parents, sisters, brothers, and friends, to embrace a life dear to him, a way of life gone forever, lost in the wind, lost in time long ago but never to leave his mind until he leaves this life. The life he had to embrace, to love in order to survive with his family will haunt him for the rest of his life.

Keep crying, old man, and embrace your beautiful memories of back in the day. Keep crying, old man, and keep going to that magnificent, enchanting, and mesmerizing world of yours. Never stop crying, old man. Never stop crying, old man, and keep going to the past. Keep going, and never stop dreaming, old man, of your wonderful, unbelievable, and remarkable past.

PROLOGUE

Incredible, Mexican Cotton Pickers back in the Day

Why was it so important to become a milero? Well, it was something bold, impressive, amazing, and incomparable; it was picking cotton to the extreme. It was like getting into a zone and feeling powerful picking so much cotton. It was amazing, and it drew recognition and praise from your family and other pickers.

The cotton pickers started to call pickers mileros if they reached the mark—picking a thousand pounds of cotton in one day. Mileros were ingenious and determined hard workers who were extremely obedient to their art of pulling cotton. This was our life back then, and the cotton fields became the way to make a living.

We were relentless, almost too proud, to just pull cotton. We were like brave young men who battled cotton always trying to reach that magical and invincible barrier, the one-thousand-pound mark. That gave us notoriety and respect in our camps, families, and particularly ourselves. Reaching that goal made us feel important and gave us a feeling of being special, people to be admired as fantastic cotton pickers by other pickers. A milero was on a mission to defeat the cotton by stamina and willpower; he was an extremist in the way he pulled cotton. Reaching the goal of picking one thousand pounds of cotton in a day made him want to go for more and keep going, keep competing with other mileros to be the best in the camp, the king of the hill day after day, week after week, and inspire other pickers with their unbelievable drive.

Becoming a milero took years beginning around age six. When you were around ten, you were pulling over five hundred pounds of cotton a day. You were inspired by family members who became mileros; you wanted to be like them. You looked up to them and followed their footsteps. You waited for the moment of your greatness. You wanted to get to the marker too; there was no letting up over the years until you got there. Pulling cotton was very demanding work, but you had many years to perfect the art and get used to the punishment your body took—the struggle, sweat, hard labor, tears, and near misses. You strove to believe and become somebody special in your camp, in your own mind.

It took many years of unbelievably laborious work, discipline, and the will to never give up before you crossed that seemingly invincible marker. And after you got there, you realized getting there was not enough and you did not want to stop. It became part of you to go to the unknown, whatever was on the side of that marker. Your feelings became greater—how far you could go, how much punishment your body could take—so you worked harder and harder until you reached the untiring heights and earned recognition and respect from your family and others. That was our real marker. *Maybe it was what we were searching for all those years—the admiration and praise of our parents and other pickers.*

Pickers had specially designed sacks; they moved so fast, not letting up. They withstood so much physical punishment pulling cotton almost to exhaustion to earn distinction, self-pride, excitement, and inner jubilation. They became addicted to the adrenaline, the sense of joy that came with their way of life. They felt unique, supreme. Those feelings were their rewards.

The importance of getting there time after time gave us hope, a feeling of pride. We could not escape this way of life because without it we could not survive.

I saw mileros laboring all day headstrong, reaching, struggling, forcing their powerful will and pride and pushing their bodies to the extremes. It was a labor of pride; they were mileros, originals, unyielding to their brutal way of life. They were unique women and men undaunted by the uncivilized hard work who became very highly skilled cotton pickers.

For mileros, there was only one way to pull cotton—hard, fast, and relentlessly. They were mileros; they never became demoralized. They never degraded the art they lived for; they yearned to reach the mark and earn respect for doing so.

They sacrificed so much of their youth, adolescence, and education so their families could have better lives. They immersed themselves in punishment because they were mileros who gave their all and more trying to reach a pinnacle in their lives.

We sacrificed so much and worked so hard to achieve a magical goal that was almost impossible for others to comprehend. The satisfaction of getting there was the reward for ourselves and our families. We could put food on the table, pay our bills, and make it through the year.

We mileros had gears—slow, fast, faster, and super-fast. We would start together, and some would gain momentum and leave others behind. I would finish my row, weigh my sack, climb the ladder, and empty my sack. I would start another row and meet the workers I had left behind, the slow ones.

Mileros start by bending over a cotton plant; as they pick, they move their left foot first just like walking. But as the sack gets heaver, they move like boxers. They push off with their right foot and their hands pick cotton; they repeat this thousands of times a day, millions of times in a lifetime. After many years of picking cotton, it becomes easier, you become better and better, and then you want to become great. You go for that magical goal, a thousand pounds in one day. You get into the way a milero thinks. Getting over that thousand-pound mark is so fulfilling; it makes you want to pull more and more until the day is over.

When the day is over and you go home, you know you have done something great, your body is feeling just wondrous but aching all over. Your self-esteem is high, and you are ready for the next day, week, month, and year—many years—to come. You have become a great cotton picker and know this is your life. So, you keep going and going to a better future.

This was our little world. Sometimes, it lasted for years. Sometimes, it lasted a lifetime. What a life we had; cotton fields gave us a way to survive. The work was laborious, but it gave us grit and pride in who we were and maybe an escape to another way of life. For the time being, working in cotton fields was insanity but our only hope too.

Was it worth it working so hard just to become a milero? Yes. What more could you ask than achieving greatness among others who did the same? That greatness was an inner greatness that exceeded your wildest dreams. We were Mexicans fighting for our survival; **we were the nomads of the cotton fields.** To Anglos, we were outsiders, unlikeable, dumb, lazy Mexicans, good-for-nothing people who picked cotton, undesirables. We had to travel the road of hate, injustice, and discrimination, but that did not stop us; it gave us fortitude and the will to continue no matter how hard it was and no matter what barriers we encountered. Our tough road was our road of hope, so we pushed our bodies to exhaustion and resigned ourselves to this way of making a living. We were unwilling to give up. We were a proud family.

And then just like that, with the invention of the cotton harvesting machines, this little world of ours in the cotton fields ended. We never again went for that marker, felt the excitement and stimulation, milero status, and felt that supreme feeling of accomplishment. Just like that, it was over. It vanished before our eyes. Part of me would stay in the cotton fields. How could I forget those monumental times and what we had to go through just to eat? All those years of working so hard—were they all for nothing?

When I was eighteen with no schooling, the only future I had foreseen was lost in the wind. The family was leaving this way of making a living after twenty years, and we were going in different directions searching for other ways to make a living. I did not have a direction, but there was a war going on, and sooner or later, I would be called up. Many cotton pickers were going to Vietnam. They had sacrificed so much in their lives for meager livings. They were then sacrificing their lives for their beloved state of Texas and the country. Those same good-for-nothing, lazy Mexicans who were not allowed to eat in many restaurants, shop in many stores, and go to go into other places were going to be fighting to safeguard the rights of people who didn't respect their rights.

When the last mileros leave this earth, their greatness will remain and never perish. When you read or hear the word *mileros*, think of great cotton pickers who gave their all for better lives for their families. Yes, you may never see that word in history books, but mileros know what it means. Memories fade, but mileros have their memories deeply implanted. No one can take away their great moments in the cotton fields, which were extraordinary, God-given gifts to them. It will never leave them until their passing, and even then, the clothes that will cover them will be made of cotton. What more could we ask for but to be buried with our friendly adversary, cotton, which gave us a chance to prove ourselves? We were not lazy, good-for-nothing Mexicans; we had dreams of a better life for our families and our people. To most, it was just a dream, but it gave us hope. The millions of Mexicans who worked in cotton fields left their mark on the winds of long ago with their accomplishments and stories.

1

CHAPTER

Onboard to Vietnam

As I was boarding the airplane, I stopped at the final step and turned around for one last look. Reality was setting in. *Will I ever see the USA again?* I asked myself. Maybe in fulfilling my service to my country, I was thinking too much about my own fate. I was excited and proud and jovial. But fear was setting in too. Many thoughts and uncertainties flashed by me. I feared the unknown, but I knew this would be an amazing time in my life.

I was going to war, flying to another country where young men were getting killed. The great thing was that I was not flying alone, hundreds of soldiers from many parts of the country were going with me. Our plane made many refueling stops. The anticipation was frightful at times as it took us more than thirty hours to get there.

In the early sixties, the war started as a small conflict, but then, hundreds of thousands of soldiers were there, and we were on our way to join them. We got closer to Vietnam with every hour. I felt overwhelmed during the trip and wondered what would happen to me. I had so many thoughts, and some were bad. This was all new. I was alone in my thoughts trying to make sense of them and trying to understand why this cotton picker had volunteered. *Martiniano, are you doing the right thing?* But there was no turning back.

Growing up, I had had dreams of going to war for my country, and my father would tell me, "Son, the greatest honor in life is to serve your country." When I turned eighteen, he took me to the registration board. I saw he was so proud. I was his fourth son who would serve our country.

1

When I was leaving for Vietnam, with tears rolling down his face, he said, "Son if you get killed over there, we will miss you but will honor you as our hero, and that's a promise." My dad saying those words made me realize that I meant a lot to him and that by going to Vietnam, I was representing my family, my heritage, my Texas, and my country.

My dad's father had fought in the Mexican Revolution when Dad was just eight. He wanted to serve in World War II but was turned down because he had nine kids. So, I was going to war, and he was so proud of me because I was trying to fulfill his dreams. I wanted to make my parents and especially my dad proud.

All the soldiers on my flight were strangers to me; we had gathered in Oakland, California, from all parts of the country. Thousands of soldiers waited for their names to be called and to board flights for Vietnam. We felt a bond, fellowship, and trust; we were in this together. Most of the soldiers were young and happy but uncertain of what lay ahead. The army became my new home; it represented an opportunity for a better life if I made it back. I wanted to find out for myself the meaning of war, I wanted to find the road to my destiny.

We came from diverse cities, towns, and ranches and were going to Vietnam for different reasons. Most had volunteered to go. I volunteered to go to Vietnam rather than remain stationed in Germany. This was a rite of passage for me, a way to test myself. I wanted to experience being there. I had dreamed of this day after having seen too many war movies. I felt called to serve just as other young Mexicans felt they had to do though many would never return.

This was my war, and I did not want to miss out. I had witnessed discrimination and hostility toward my family and myself many times because of being Mexican while I was traveling and working in the fields in Texas. Mexicans were not allowed in most restaurants and many other places in most parts of Texas. Thousands of Mexicans and Mexican Americans had fought in most wars for America, but in many states, that did not matter; discrimination continued, and we were considered undesirable, ugly, dumb, good-for-nothing Mexicans. We were undaunted. We still went by the hundreds of thousands from all over the nation because we were Americans too.

We wanted to prove we were as much American as any others were and more. We were willing to put our lives on the line because we felt it was our duty. I wanted to be part of this war because I had been born in this country, and whatever happened before would never change because they could not change my Mexican heritage. Many Mexican Americans from my hometown and all over the Rio Grande Valley went to war and faced its dangers knowing that many would not be coming back.

After flying for many hours, reading magazines, and talking and bonding with other soldiers, boredom set in, and I reflected on my transformation from a shy young, stuttering boy to the person I'd become. I had spent most of my years traveling to the cotton fields, and then the army made me a soldier prepared for war. I had gone through twelve weeks of basic training—running, marching, firing rifles and machine guns. Then, I went to the Chemical Warfare School in Fort McClellan, Alabama, and learned how to handle flamethrowers, which was exciting.

The army gave me another perspective; all the young men serving with me were from different races and backgrounds. I did not feel out of place; I felt like somebody who was learning a lot. It was a wonderful time in my life. These young men were no better than me, and I was no better than them. I was going through unbelievable changes and discovering new things every day. There was an eagerness, an excitement in my new world, so different from the cotton fields I had worked on a year and a half earlier. I was a former cotton picker on a plane with challenges awaiting, but I was not worried about them. I had had to face danger in the cotton fields, and I had come close to death twice.

Traveling to another country was not a new experience for me; the army had sent me to Germany at first but I had not liked it there because we American soldiers stationed there were not wanted. I volunteered to go to Vietnam because I wanted to. Germany was cold. I wanted warmth. And there was a war going on I wanted to be part of. Something in my mind was forcing me there; I could not help it. I knew I would face danger, but that did not matter. I wanted to see and feel the war for myself.

I loved being in the army. Wearing my uniform gave me a great feeling of pride, passion, and respect for it. I was meeting soldiers from other backgrounds, different races, and all parts of the country, and I was discovering they were just like me. Prior to that, all my friends had been Mexicans. Having many white and black friends and others was a first for me. I was treated with respect. We were all equal; the color of my skin or being Mexican did not matter. I had stepped into a world I had not known existed, and I felt I could be somebody there, a human being. That was great for my self-esteem, and I was at peace knowing we were all in this together and willing to fight as one.

Getting out of my shell and on my own was a great learning experience. I had come from another world, the world of migrant workers living nomadic existences traveling from town to town. *Is the army a make-believe world? No. I'm not dreaming. This is real. I have learned so much this year and am glad to be in the army. Nobody is sending me to Vietnam but myself.* I had no regrets. I was doing the right thing. Yes, I did not have many options; I had had little schooling, but the army would be my school and my hope for a better life. I was following my instincts and hoping and praying this road was the right one. Many feelings were going through me—excitement, anxiety, pride, passion— but I felt I had to relax and be in control of myself.

2
===== CHAPTER

Flying with My Little Brother

It was an overwhelming trip—a day and a half of flying. Flying was unreal, awesome; I felt like Superman. I wondered what was going through the other soldiers' minds. *Are they scared? Are they feeling the same weight I am?* Seeing them gave me a feeling of security, strength, and tremendous pride; we were so many though we knew soldiers were being killed over there, but flying with them gave me confidence and a sense of pride. I was scared, but we all were. We were hundreds of soldiers flying while hundreds of thousands were already there.

I went back and forth in my mind trying to reconcile with my ex-girlfriend, family, and friends that I may have hurt; I asked them for their forgiveness in this stage of my life. I thought of all those I loved. I was flying close to the heavens; my past was coming in flashes. The thought that I might not make it back made me fearful.

So much going through me—flashes of so many faces of past good and bad times. I was reliving them, trying to cleanse myself, and confessing to God before I arrived in case I did not make it back. I remembered my achievements, disappointments, and regrets and asked for forgiveness for my mistakes. I prayed a lot. I would face enemies who did not know I already hated them. This was all new—going to war and hating others I did not know.

Then my thoughts took me back to my fascination with the world of cotton fields. I wanted to relive my past regrets and fears and the unforgettable years of my earlier life. What a life we had lived—years in the fields and all the traveling. On the plane, I was so far removed from my past. It seemed so long ago, but it was not my fascination with cotton fields; the biggest part was that they had become my hiding place ~ my security blanket. They had given me hope and time to conquer and heal my insecurities as I was growing up. I always felt secure and happy working in the cotton fields. Reminiscing, I was now in my make-believe world picking cotton.

I needed and wanted to return to my past and wanted my younger brother Apollonio beside me. In my mind, we were together in the cotton fields. He knew the meaning of family going through those tough but wonderful years. Having my younger brother with me in my make-believe world, we relived the world of the cotton picker time and again. I would tell him our life stories in the fields; they were not illusions but real and true events then. I wanted him to find out what we had gone through. I needed to share my passage of life with him since I was flying close to the heavens and wanted to reinforce the love I had for him. I knew these were only thoughts—my little brother, Apollonio, was no longer living except in my thoughts and sometimes in my dreams. There, I would take him with me wherever I went.

3
CHAPTER

Apollonio

I have never forgotten him. My younger brother, Apollonio. He died when he was only about a year old. I missed him so much. It hurt not having a little brother I could play with and talk to and join me in the cotton fields. I had six older brothers, four older sisters, and a younger sister. He was a missing part in my life; there was an empty sadness in my heart. I wanted him to sense the feeling of belonging to the family.

I will confess one thing. One day when I was carrying Apollonio around, he slipped from my hands and fell and hit the floor; he cried. Mom picked him up. Then, all I could remember was seeing him in a small white coffin. I did not understand what he was doing in there and why he was not moving. All I wanted was to play with him but he would not move. Mom made me understand he had died and gone to heaven, a place far up in the sky. As I was growing up, I felt guilty because I thought I had caused his death. Mom told me that he had died because he was sick, but I still blamed myself and carried that guilt for many years until I understood better.

I wanted to tell Apollonio all about my life ~ adventures, recollections, stories, and the history of our family. I wanted him to know about and relish the times we had been through—the memorable times, even the depressing times, and the wonderful places we traveled to so far away from home. All the housing we had to endure and live in. The people we met, and all the hard work, and our many good times we shared as a family. I wanted to make up for all he had missed. I could him ~ I would tell him.

So, Apollonio, here are my stories and some of the history of our family.

Let me start with a funny story that happened when I was around five years old. I still drank milk in a bottle, and Mommy wanted to change that; she wanted me to drink milk from a glass, but I did not want that. I wanted a bottle, a bottle I would make myself. I would get a can of pet milk, put it in two bottles with some water and sugar, and shake them. I would give one to my younger sister, Tillie. Then I would go into my room, lie on the bed, cross my legs, and drink my milk.

One day, I went into the kitchen but could not find the milk bottles. When I went to tell Mom about that, she said she had seen a taquache, a possum, with the bottles and had chased him out; he had gone under our house. I went out to look and came back. "I looked, Mom, but I didn't see any taqauche."

"He's somewhere under the house. I'll give you a glass of milk," she said.

"No! I want my milk bottle!" I replied.

"Well, you'll have to go under the house and get it."

"I will, Mom."

I went out and crawled under the house—no bottles, no taqauche. I was dirty all over, and I was mad. I thought, *When I see him, I'll get my father's rifle and shoot him, yes. I hate him.* I went inside, and Mom said, "Son, you need a shower."

"Oh no I don't."

"Oh yes you do!"

Into the shower I went. There was no milk bottle for my sister or me.

Well, Apollonio, years later, Mother told me, "Martin, there was never a taquache. I got rid of the milk bottles because you were too old. Not your sister, but we had to take hers too because then you would have taken her bottle." She laughed. But she was right.

8

4

CHAPTER

Truckers

"Lupe Trevino, with his dog overlooking the cotton patch."

I can't forget my heroes of yesteryear ~ the Truckers. They were not movies stars or war heroes, but they were heroes to all the migrant workers and their families. They helped for the betterment of thousands of Mexican families. By their deeds, they helped many families carve out a living. They were our leaders. Most did not have schooling, but they had experience and smarts. People would follow them. The truckers provided work and opportunities for people to make the money they needed to support their families.

These truckers would pick up the migrant workers from their homes, stopping at eight to ten homes, before driving to the fields. They'd work hard picking alongside us and when the work was done for the day, they'd take everyone home ~ thus getting back to their homes even later.

When the work was finished in one town, the truckers would migrate on to another town. They would travel hundreds of miles and at times to other states too. They knew the way and where we could find work.

They were also there in times of need. If someone was sick or hurt the truckers would take them to the hospital or doctor. They would give rides into town so that people could buy groceries and supplies. When trouble arose, they were there to help drive us to a safer place. When a special event was happening in town, they would help people get there.

I grew up seeing these men in my town of Edinburg Texas; in my neighborhood. I'd see them fixing their trucks getting them ready ~ constantly prepared. My dad was one of these truckers. He was a great leader. I helped him work on his trucks and he taught me so much not only about trucks but about life.

Some nights when my mind goes back to yesteryear, I can still hear the sounds of the trucks ~ the roar from the engines passing by my house. They have been forgotten, lost in time, lost in the past. However, without them, our lives would have been so much harder, less rewarding, and we wouldn't have had the steppingstone to move forward. They were heroes to many Mexican families.

5

================= CHAPTER

First Time Picking Cotton

When I was about six, most of our family was working in the cotton fields. Only Mom, my younger sister, and I were left at home. Mom, I want to go pick cotton. "Can I, Mom? Look—I've already made my own cotton sack." It was more like a small bag, three feet long with a strap, and the bottom was closed.

"Son, you're too young. You could get lost there," she said.

"Mom, Dad will look after me."

"Well, son, your daddy is coming for lunch in a few minutes. Ask him."

A little later, I saw Dad coming. *Here's my chance.* "Dad, look. I made a cotton sack!"

"That's nice, son."

"Can you take me to the cotton fields so I can try it out?"

"Son, you're too young."

"I am not!"

Mother had overheard the conversation. "Take him. He's been after me all morning."

"I must do my work in peace, but okay, I'll take him after lunch."

So Dad took me to work, where I saw Benito, my brother. Dad had a large crew picking cotton, and I saw that our truck was almost full of cotton. I got out of the car with my sack in hand and was ready to pick cotton.

Dad said, "There is your cotton you can pick."

I stood next to a cotton row looking at all that cotton; the stalks came

11

up to my face. I was not moving. I had never picked cotton before. I looked at Dad helplessly.

"Son, this is the way you pick with your fingers and pull the cotton. Then you put it into your sack."

Cotton is an open, fluffy, soft, white flower. I picked slowly using both hands. When my sack was full, I brought it back, and Dad, who had left me alone but had watched me, weighed it. "Six pounds. That's good, son."

I was happy and having fun picking cotton with my family. I took a sack full of cotton and climbed up the ladder at the back of the truck that contained lots of cotton. It looked so soft and fluffy that I emptied my sack, jumped into the cotton, and rolled around. I was having so much fun. A little girl jumped in as well. We were laughing and having fun, but then as I was jumping, I felt a sharp pain in my stomach. I knew what it was right away.

I went down the ladder to the ground and looked around. I tried to unbuckle my belt, but it was too tight. Realizing number two was coming fast, I was looking for a place to do it, but there were people all over, so I went under the truck by the tires, and all hell broke loose. My face turned red. I was devastated. Shit was flowing down my legs, and I cried like a child. Dad heard me and came over to me. "What happened, son?" he asked.

"I shit my pants, Daddy."

"I see." He called out to Benito, "Come over here. Take your brother back home. He just shit his pants." Dad was laughing, and Benito was too.

"Get in the back of the pickup," Benito told me. I climbed into the pickup bed and was not alone; by then, lots of flies were swarming around me. Off we went.

Back home, Benito told me to get out and wait next to the truck. He got a water hose and sprayed me all over. He loosened my belt, took off my pants, and sprayed me again. Mom came out with a towel. "Dry yourself, then go in the house to change clothes. Your brother will take you back to the cotton field to pick more cotton, right?"

"No, Mom. I don't want to pick any more cotton. I'm tired. I'll take a nap."

There was no way I would go back there and face the workers who had heard about my troubles, and there was no way I could face that little girl.

That was my first experience picking cotton—six pounds of it and about a pound of shit. I did not know what happened to my sack but did not care. I had had some fun, though that was my first disappointment, my first embarrassment. Yes, maybe there was a future for me in those cotton fields, but first, I needed a better belt and a new sack.

6

$=$ CHAPTER

Working in the Fields

"Martín explaining to his grandson how he picked
cotton and collected it in a sack."

Picking cotton was like being in another world; we traveled to many towns and met people who were not like us. They spoke English, and we could as well, but we were more comfortable with Spanish, and our mother spoke only Spanish. The townspeople were mostly white. We were technically white too but of Mexican heritage. We had to travel hundreds of miles to work in cotton fields to survive.

Every year, we went on the cotton trail, moving north as the cotton was ready to be picked. We would start in South Texas and end in the north near the panhandle. We would go through Amarillo, Lubbock, Wellington, Clarendon, Childress, Temple, Quail, Midland, and many more towns—hundreds of towns.

We also picked cotton in many states—Oklahoma New Mexico, California, and Arizona—but mostly in Texas. Not all cotton fields were the same; in Arizona, the cotton plants were the tallest. I did not like that; I could not pick as fast, and it was too hot. I preferred the panhandle of Texas, where cotton plants were three feet tall, in some cases they were close to the ground.

My main schooling was in the fields; my teachers were my parents, brothers, and sisters learning the best ways to pick cotton. Yes, anybody can pick cotton, but to be great at it took many years of hard and dedicated work and learning the tricks of the trade. Every year, I learned better ways to pick cotton, something I still cherish knowing. I spend most of my youth and my teen years picking cotton from June through October and some times into November or December.

After the first freeze the leaves turn brown and fall off. By this time the cotton balls had opened up but the ones that didn't open died. Some cotton rows are longer than others depending on the landscape. After mid-November, the weather would get cold, sometimes very cold, and many years, we picked through the Christmas holidays. That was a little bitter. It was a time when other people were shopping for gifts, but we did not complain. We understood we were not on vacation. Though we picked during many Christmas seasons, our parents bought us gifts. Sometimes, we celebrated Christmas in Edinburg if we had earned enough for the nonworking months. Dad would always point to cotton fields and say, "Look at all that money out there. Just pick it and it's yours." He always tried hard to motivate us and give us confidence. We knew what he was doing, but we knew he was very proud of the whole family, the older mileros and mileras and the younger ones equally.

When I was young, my sack was ten feet long. Later, I carried a twelve and then a fourteen-foot sack. The more I picked, the stronger my legs became and the more my whole body got used to all the hard work. After many years, it became effortless and easier.

My sack became an extension of myself. I took good care of it and repaired it as necessary. They were fourteen feet long with pieces of wire to keep them open; we did not even have to look; we knew the cotton we were throwing into them was going into them. We lined the underside of our sacks with material to protect the sacks from the hard dirt and sometimes sticks on the ground. They were tied shut at the far end, so, we could untie that end when we were dumping our sacks into the trailer; that made it quicker to unload a fourteen-foot sack. And we made sure our shoulder straps were wide and padded to protect our shoulders from stress. We put hooks in front of the straps to make it easier to unload them. Dad taught us to mix flour and water into a paste and coat the undersides of our sacks with that. It cut down on the friction of dragging sacks. My family's sacks were a main reason that no other families could pick like us. No one could have become a milero or milera without such tricks of the trade.

I would attack the cotton, picking hard all day, getting into a zone. It was amazing how much cotton you could pick on those days. It was hard pulling the sack all day—bending, repetitive motions, weighing sacks fifteen times, going up the ladder fifteen times, but when you were in a zone, you could do it and feel indescribable joy and fulfillment. We welcomed rivalry; it was our nourishment, our source of pride.

In winter, I used to wear long johns under my pants, and I would wear two shirts, a sweater, and a jacket. As the day went on, I would take my jacket off and then perhaps my sweater when it got warmer, and that made picking easier.

On Saturdays we would go into town. It was great—shopping and movies made up for working hard all week. Sometimes, I wondered if we were poor. I did not think so because we ate well and had a house, truck, cars, and other nice things. Yes, every year we traveled to make a living. It was a tough life, but I had been born into it, and I loved picking with my family.

The Chapa family learned to absorb all the hard work and punishment of the cotton fields with discipline, determination, and pride. We reached our goals and relished the sense of accomplishment. We conquered cotton every day we picked. We saw money in the fields we picked; it was our way to a better life. That kept us going and overpowering cotton. At times, I took my passion and pride out on the cotton, and the work became effortless. Working with older members of the family gave me a sense of togetherness. I felt protected; I loved my family very much, so working with them was great. We had strong bonds. The pride and the love we had for each other—what more could I ask for? The fact that I was with my family made up for the rough work all those months away from home. Seeing my brothers and sisters pulling cotton and going beyond the pain had a powerful influence on me; I wanted to imitate them. I could not match their resourcefulness, but I knew that someday I would. I tried to be like them for the betterment of the family. Pulling cotton as a family was so special and rewarding that the hard work did not bother us. I loved the work and the life of a cotton picker. I was sure that would be my future.

7

══════════ CHAPTER

The Exorcism

I was being held down on the grass on top of a cross made of flour. I had been stripped of my clothes. I was yelling, kicking, and crying. People were saying words over me; they wanted to cure my stuttering with this strange remedy. I was so embarrassed.

They finished, and I ran into the house. I went to bed crying until I fell asleep with flour all over me. Well, that remedy did not work. I continued stuttering. I think it got worse. Sometimes, I sounded like a machine-gun going *t-t-t-t-t-t-t* before I could get a word out. Life was not getting better because of my stuttering. *What's wrong with me? Why is this happening?* I could not figure it out. It was only a stutter, but my biggest fear was not being able to speak like my brothers and sisters. Sometimes, there so much I wanted to say, but the words would not come out. It was as if something in me was keeping my words from coming out.

I cried many nights trying to understand, trying to make sense if it. *Why do I have this problem?* My stuttering was holding me back. Many times when I wanted to use many different, bigger words but could not, I had to resort to smaller words or I could not speak. The only time I was not stuttering was in my dreams or thoughts. I never stuttered when I was thinking and not every time I spoke. But I would stutter most of the time, and the fear of stuttering was always there. I was afraid to speak, fearful of the stuttering, and it was terrifying.

As I got older, I fought hard to defeat my stuttering, and little by little, I was winning the battle, but that took many years. By clenching my stomach muscles as I spoke, I was able to kind of control some of my stuttering, and that was promising. In my make-believe world, there was no stuttering. In it, I hid my fears and shyness and stayed balanced. I imagined good things in life and protection from my fears and bad things. I could be whatever I wanted to be and do anything in my magical, make-believe world of dreams, my refuge from the outside world.

8
CHAPTER

Edinburg

Edinburg was hot—very hot. We would pick until lunch, and it would be so hot then that you could cook an egg on the hood of a truck. We rested then for an hour under a truck or trees for protection from the blazing sun. The temperature often reached a hundred, and I would be sweating under the relentless sun. Our only relief was clouds and cold water that we would drink and pour on our backs. That helped until the sun dried out our clothes. Sometimes, lying motionless on a sack helped a bit. By three thirty, the sun was less hot. What got us through days of unbearably hard work was our mind-set, the energy we drew from our inner selves. We had little choice in the matter because we had to earn money, and I was grateful for the opportunity to do that. Not every day was miserable, but most of them were. I started work at a fast pace, and I would slow down after lunch until things got a bit cooler. I picked up my pace knowing I would be going home in a few more hours. We wore long-sleeved shirts for protection from the cotton branches, but there was no protection from the sun whether you were picking or standing still.

At the end of the summer, we would follow the cotton harvest all the way to the panhandle, over six hundred miles away. We stopped in many small towns and picked cotton until late December or early January. The work was very demanding and sometimes even dangerous, but it was our livelihood. We worked as a group; this was our bread and butter, our way of life.

We made the most money picking cotton for four to five months a year; our family worked half a year so we could survive the other half of the year. Pulling cotton in South Texas was hard because of the hot weather, and the most you pick in one day was around five hundred pounds. But as we got closer to the panhandle, the cotton was heavier and pulling cotton was better, and after a few months, the weather got cooler—perfect for pulling cotton.

9
CHAPTER

Maria

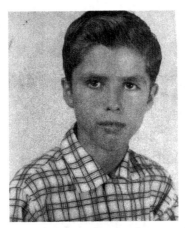

"Martín's 4th grade school picture."

I was around ten and at school. We were outside with one teacher. We were racing, boys and girls, and I was fast. I was ahead of everyone. Just before crossing the finish line, I slowed down, and I saw a flash go by me. I looked and saw that a girl with long hair had beaten me. At first, I was upset. I approached her as she was lying on the grass and breathing hard. She smiled at me. She was beautiful. I asked her for her name, and she said it was Maria.

From then on, we were together at recess everyday holding hands. I went early to school to play jacks with her. I was so happy being with her. I wondered if this was love. I didn't know, but I knew I had a nice feeling for her. When school ended for the year, we said goodbye, "See you next year!"

The following year, I attended another school and never saw Maria again, but her beauty and smile stayed with me. I'll never forgot the girl who beat me in a race and stole something from me. I remember her smile, her beauty, and her name, *Maria*.

10
CHAPTER

Jim

By about age ten I was pulling over five hundred pounds of cotton a day, *ten dollars*. That was one reason our and many thousands of other families took their children to the cotton fields. Picking cotton was difficult, and we picked for many months; that meant we missed a lot of school, but the families had no other choice.

I will always remember spending four weeks at one place picking cotton; those were the longest, scariest, and worst weeks of my life. We got to a house that was in terrible condition. Grass had grown up all around it, and it was dusty and dirty.

The women immediately started cleaning the inside while the men cleaned up the outside. My brother Javier found a well outside. It was very dark. My dad got a rope and a flashlight. Dad tied the rope around my brother's waist, and he climbed down. A dead animal was at the bottle of the well. But we needed the water to shower and clean the house. We shared that house with two other families. Everybody moved their belongings in and settled in.

Dad told Mom he would see Jim, who owned the place, about the cotton fields. Dad asked me if I wanted to come, and I said yes. We got to Jim's house, and Dad knocked on the door. Jim, a white man, came out. He asked my dad if I was his son. "Yes," my father said. "He is Martin, one of twelve."

"Wow! That's a big family," Jim said. "Since you have a very big family, why not let me have this little one?"

I was sure the guy was crazy, and I could tell Dad did not like him.

He went on; he said he would take good care of me and send me to school. He said that I would have a very nice home and that one day it would be mine. *Is this guy joking? I hate this gringo.* Dad just laughed and got the information for the cotton field; we went home, and Dad told Mom what Jim had said. Mom laughed too, but I was scared. *What if they give me away to Jim? Dad and Mom would never give me away, would they? No, they wouldn't.*

Monday came along, and we started picking. A few hours later, Jim drove up in his pickup and talked with Dad. I wondered if they were talking about me. I was scared. I was so unhappy. I suspected my parents, and I was going through a miserable time. There were nights that I just could not sleep because I was worried about being left with Jim.

Finally, we finished all of Jim's cotton fields and left. My fears of being left with Jim had been all in my head. I was happy again; there was joy in my life again as we traveled to a new place, no Jim. I felt reborn. What a relief. That was the last time I saw Jim. Thinking of him while we were there had distracted me terribly, but I learned never to mistrust my parents again. They loved me too much to leave me behind.

11

CHAPTER

Father

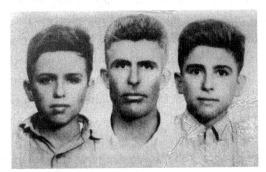

"My dad with Israel and Felix in 1943."

"My dad with me horseback riding."

"My dad circa 1950's."

My dad's name was Martiniano Chapa. I was named after him. He was born in Mexico. He married my mother, Paulina Ybarra, in South Texas. They went to Mexico, where he had a farm. He worked it for over ten years before he and his two sons, Felix and Israel, returned to the States to get work so the rest of our family could come. My mother came with seven children to Texas in 1944 and settled in Edinburg Texas, where Olga, I, and Otilia were born. Nine children were born in Mexico and four in Texas.

Dad was a very smart, well respected, and wonderful man. He planned all the trips every year. He knew many owners of cotton fields and how long it took to pick their cotton. We lived on a busy street in Edinburg when we weren't picking cotton. My father would gather other pickers for four or five months of picking cotton. He chose only good pickers who were hard working and dependable.

Dad got $2 per hundred pounds of cotton, so he offered some pickers $1.50 per hundred pounds. Others were gathering crews as well, and some offered more money, and some pickers wanted shorter trips so their children would not miss that much school. Others did not want short trips; they just wanted to pick. Others wanted all the details on housing, so many things had to be worked out.

At night, I slept by the windrow facing the street and heard trucks passing by. Some stopped at the railroad tracks in the next neighborhood looking for cotton pickers. There were so many trucks; some were ten wheelers bigger and heavier than our six-wheel truck. The whole area was busy with men in trucks going up and down the streets looking for workers and girls and stopping to talk with other drivers. After a few days, our town got quiet; most truckers had found their people and had left. In many neighborhoods, homes were boarded up when the owners went to pick cotton.

During these times, Dad was out every night looking for the better workers, and most times, he found them. Before we left, Dad put wooden arches across the truck bed and covered them with canvas to protect the family from wind, rain, sun, and cold. We rode in the back of the truck with some tables, chairs, stoves, beds, clothing, pots, pans, and other belongings of the families coming with us.

Our dad was an excellent leader. He could cook, and he knew everything about farming, dealing with animals, and people. He was always positive; he joked a lot, and he sang. There was almost nothing he could not do. When he said it time to go, we went. We were always excited about leaving. So many families were doing the same and heading for many parts of Texas and other states every year after picking cotton in the area in hot weather.

We wanted cooler weather, but it was hard leaving the comforts of our home. We had to go, however; this journey had to be taken, and more than half the families in Edinburg and the Rio Grande Valley were going to difference places. Thousands of people migrated for work. Our family spent many months living away from home. Some families picked until school started, but others, including my family, stayed through the holidays and some years even longer.

One time, I saw a picker with the longest bag I had ever seen; it weighed twenty pounds all by itself. My dad would deduct that weight from the total weight of the bag and cotton in it. Dad had a book in which he kept track of each person's name, date, and weights of sacks, and the pickers kept duplicate books. On Saturdays, Dad would be paid by the owners of the fields and would in turn pay the workers.

My sisters or I would add all the totals of each person or family. If a family picked five thousand pounds of cotton for the week, they were paid $100, $2 per every hundred pounds. After that, we went to town to relax and have a good time. On Sundays, we repaired our sacks as needed. Dad was our leader in that regard; he was very good at sewing and repairing the sacks, and my sisters and brothers and I would join in; it was great being together. Sometimes, we did not work during the week because of rain, so that meant we would work on Saturdays and sometimes on Sundays, but that was rare. Because our work was so hard, we needed time off.

Those who owned trucks were very important; thousands depended on them. One was Renteria. His brother had been paralyzed from the waist down and walked with crutches. He was always smiling and happy. Renteria always took a family by the name of Lopez. My dad always tried to get the Lopezes to join him because one of their sons was a great picker. Benito and I wanted him to come with us; the three of us had pulled cotton around Edinburg many times. Benito always picked more cotton than us, but the three of us made a great trio. We wanted the Lopez family because the cotton was better by the panhandle; if he came, we would race every day, and I was still young. Benito always took the lead helping Neto with the cotton roll, and Neto helped me. We stayed close together, getting energy from each other. But Neto's father was committed to Renteria, so every year, Neto's family went with him.

My best friend lived behind our house just a fence away. I spent many days with the sons of the Soto family playing ball and all kinds of games. Many times, I would see Lupe Trevino, the dad, and brother-in-law Ben working on their trucks getting them ready to pick oranges, melons, onions, lettuce, peppers, and then cotton depending on the season. These men would find work from the farmers and go looking for workers they would drive to and from the fields Monday through Friday and sometimes on Saturday, but Saturday was mostly spent paying the workers, going out to town, shopping, eating, and going to the movies. On Sundays, we went to church, relaxed, saw more movies, and fixed the trucks. Dad would take me along to pay the workers, and we went to many houses. That was life back then. The traveling was never the same. Some years, it was better than others, but it was always exciting knowing that most of your friends were doing the same. It was fun even though it was months of hard work.

Sometimes, Dad would ask me to help with the truck. If he was picking oranges, a sidewall had to be taken down. The growers would supply the boxes made of wood measuring four feet by four feet and four feet tall. The workers would be given sacks like cotton sacks but smaller, about two feet long. They could be folded, and they had a hook attached to a ring around the mouth of the sack that kept it open. The sack had a strap that went over your shoulder. You could pick oranges with both hands, and when your sack was full, you would walk to the truck, where there was a worker ready to put the oranges in the boxes. You would be paid based on how often you filled the sack. It was hard going up ladders to pick oranges higher on the tree.

Thousands of Mexican families made their living working in the fields; such agricultural work was our main source of income. We made just enough money to get by. We made more on the trips we took every year to many towns in Texas.

My dad taught me many important lifelong lessons. He would give us lectures how to behave toward people. One was to always respect your elders. Another was that if you were sitting on a bus and all the seats were taken and there was someone standing, you get up and offer your seat to them. He also taught us that if you are going or coming into any place, make sure you hold open the door to the person behind you. Be kind to them and let them go in first. Always say good morning, good afternoon, thank you, or excuse me to people. Your behavior towards others must always be respectable. He told me, "Son, with your kindness and respect towards others and doing the little deeds you do, people will respond with kindness. That will enlighten you and make you grow and become a better person."

My dad was right. Once I opened the door for an old woman. She was very impressed, smiled and said to me, "Thank you young man." A feeling of warmheartedness went through me. I felt great!

Dad was always teaching me new and important things in life. He was my first teacher. I have so much respect for him.

12

$=$ **CHAPTER**

My Sister's Suitor

Dad was good at speaking Spanish and English. Many times, men who wanted to get married would ask Dad to help them. Dad would go with them to ask for the hands of the girls they wanted to marry. He was well respected; he had gone to school in Mexico and his Spanish was excellent, and most of the time, he succeeded in getting the girls for the guys. At times, however, he was told by the parents of certain girls to leave; they did not want their daughters to marry the young men Dad was speaking for.

One night, a young man and his father came to speak to Dad and Mom about their son who wanted to marry Minerva, my oldest sister. I listened to the young man asking for my sister's hand; he had a dark complexion, and my sister's complexion was very white; she was beautiful. They talked for a while until Dad said, "Well, since they both want to marry and are in love, what can I say but to give my daughter permission to marry?"

A year later, we had a big wedding with lots of food, music, and people in our backyard. It was great.

13

CHAPTER

My Grandfather

My dad was my hero. I spend a lot of time with him going to many places. I loved riding around with him; I was humbled to share his name. My dad's father, Felix Chapa had been killed when my Dad was only eight years old. My grandfather had fought as a sergeant in the Mexican Revolution and came home on leave. One night while he was home, Benito, his brother, invited him to a dance in town, but my grandfather decided not to go. Benito went to the dance, and police officers there took his gun. They said he could have it back when he left. Benito turned in his gun and went in to dance. When he left, he stopped for his gun, but the officer said he was going to keep his gun. He went home and told my grandfather about not getting his gun back. "Well, little brother," he told Benito, "a man without a gun is not a man. Let's get it back."

They went to the dance, and my grandfather went straight to the officers asking for his brother's gun. The officer in charge asked him what gun, and they went back and forth arguing until guns were drawn and bullets were flying. Benito was shot in the leg, and an officer was hit. My grandfather took Benito, and they ran out and hid under a bridge. More officers were looking for them. An old woman told the officers where they were hiding, and the officers surrounded them and told them to come out. My grandfather was holding his wounded younger brother as they came out. They were lined up at a wall and shot. They were left there; the family recovered their bodies the following morning. Felix Chapa, my grandfather, and Benito Chapa, my great-uncle, were killed because of a gun and a misunderstanding. My dad was fatherless at age eight; by age ten, he was on his own.

Dad named his firstborn son Felix after his dad, and another son Benito after his great-uncle. I never knew my grandfathers; both were gone by the time I was born.

14

CHAPTER

Baseball

Once I played little league baseball. My best friend Lupe asked me if I wanted to try out for the team. I thought, well why not. I bought a baseball glove at the 5 and 10 store for five dollars. It was not very good one but I loved it. All the other boys had better ones.

Lupe and his Uncle West picked me up. There were 13 boys trying out. Five were white and the rest were Mexican. I did great at tryouts. I threw balls hard and long. I was a fast runner and played third base. When tryouts were done, the team was picked. I did not make the team. I was cut. I felt sad. I knew that I was much better than most of the other boys.

The night of the first baseball game Lupe and his Uncle West came to my house and told me I made the team. One of the boys was too old. You had to be 12 years old. West told me to bring my birth papers so I did. They gave me a uniform. We were representing the Valley Store Yankees. My number was 7. I was thrilled to wear it. I was a player.

We got to the baseball park and started playing catch with the players getting warmed up before the game. Our coaches were Garza and my friend Lupe's Uncle West. They called me over. They were trying to decide who would pitch the first game. West got a glove and told me to throw the ball. So I threw it hard and then harder. They looked at each other and said, "This is our pitcher for tonight." I had never pitched before. We won our first game. I struck out ten players. I became the starting pitcher for our team. Just a day before I was home crying because I hadn't made the team and now I was their starting pitcher!

I loved my lucky number 7 uniform. But for my third game I didn't have it. During that game I walked the first three players. Then the next batter came up. He was a huge white boy. I pitched a hard ball down the middle of the plate. He hit it so hard that it left the park. It was so high in the sky. I turned around. I saw runners crossing home plate. I was in shock. I don't know how we finally got 3 outs on them but we did. I went into the dugout and threw my glove. I didn't want to pitch any more. West came over, put his arm around me trying to console me. He told me, "Martin, next time you go out there, throw one pitch low and the other high." So I went out and pitched one low and the other high. I closed out the inning with no runs. Then our team started to score runs. The score was now 4 to 2. The following inning I had to pitch to the huge, white boy again. By this time I knew him. On my first pitch, I went low. He missed. Then I pitched one high. He missed again. Then I pitched a low ball. Again he missed. He was out. In the last inning I had to pitch to him again. I struck him out the same as before. Finally the game was over. We won it 5 runs to 4!

Four weeks later we met the same team. Their name was the Tides. My first time batting I hit a home run. The second time I hit the fence for a triple. I was hot! My third time at bat the other team changed pitchers. It was the huge, white boy. He struck me out in three pitches and did the same the last time I was at bat. He was a great player. Both of us made it an all-star game playing together.

In our last game of the season my coach called me over. He said, "Martin it has been great having you playing on my team. At first you were cut but then we were able to have you come and join. You came back to be my best player. You should be very proud of yourself! I have picked you for the all-star game. I will be coaching. I'm going to let you choose from these two players who will be going to the game with you." I chose one. I never forgot that great year playing baseball and the words of my coach.

15

$$\text{CHAPTER}$$

Monsters in the Sky

There were monsters in the sky sometimes when the weather was just right; a beautiful blue sky with clouds forming, moving slowly overhead; you could see figures, monsters, horses, Indians, mountains—a cloud show. We'd look up and say, "Look there. That looks like a dog, and that looks like a building." We'd see jets trailing smoke as well, and sometimes rainbows.

Those were wonderful times, breaks from picking, times to relax for a little while before getting back to our little world. They say money doesn't grow on trees, but the more cotton I picked, the more money I made. Dad would say, "Look at that cotton field and all that money growing on those beautiful plants. The only thing you have to do is pick it."

Picking cotton was a repetitive motion—picking fast, pulling the sack, using both hands. First, your left would pick one or two balls of open cotton and give them to your right hand, which would throw them into your sack in one motion. You performed it thousands of times during the day every day, millions of times in your life.

After doing it for so many years, you became an exceptional, fantastic cotton picker. The better the cotton fields, the more you picked. It was nourishment when the fields were good. You got jittery, excitable, and irresistible when attacking the cotton. This was a difficult plight, but it was the only way to make money in that season.

It was a radical way of making a living; some people called it uncivilized or inhumane. But we flourished in that environment; thousands of other Mexican families were pulling cotton too. It was our way of life, of surviving, of achieving a better life, a steppingstone to a better life. We were soldiers in a war with cotton. Pulling cotton was not a disgrace but a path to salvation and moving forward as a family.

We cotton pickers were well respected; we were hard workers, and the farmers needed us as much as we need them. We depended on them as they depended on us. Our dreams were in the cotton fields for the time being. Our bodies got used to that way of life, and we developed speed, endurance, motivation, tactics, and pride. We were unwilling to be conquered by this hard way of life.

We had small dreams, make-believe dreams that kept us going with no schooling. They were in the back of our minds as we picked cotton. I had no regrets. I loved pulling cotton. I was a young boy trying to find my way, and this was the only way my parents had known.

My fascination with cotton fields started at a very early age; I saw my brothers and sisters picking cotton, and most of the people in our neighborhood did the same. The most demeaning thing about picking cotton for me was that when we finished a cotton field and had a few days left before moving to another. Dad would take us to a field that was meant to be picked by cotton harvesting machines. We would pick about ten feet from the front and back of the field. The cotton was so plentiful and so beautiful, but we could pick only ten feet. That was inconsiderate, demeaning, but we had to do it for a few days before moving to another field. The machine could then come in and adjust the blades so it could harvest the cotton much better.

Time was not on our side; the cotton harvesting machines were starting to rule, and the better cotton fields were reserved for them. It was as if certain fields were too good for us. Who knows how many hundreds of pounds of cotton we could have picked in those fields.

16

CHAPTER

Watermelon

One day, Dad told us were going to a new field with very good cotton. When we got close to the owner's house, we saw a big dog. The owner told me he was very friendly. "He'll jump on you do, but don't be afraid. He's very playful."

The owner told us of a watermelon patch by his house, and he gave us permission to eat as much as we wanted while we picked cotton. We could not wait until we got closer to the house so we could eat some watermelon.

After picking for two hours, we got closer to the house, and the big dog—the huge dog—ran and jumped on one worker after another knocking them down. He knocked over one of my sisters. The dog was going after everyone and knocking him or her down. He came straight at me and knocked me down even though I had braced myself. He licked my face and ran off. That was the last time we saw him.

Then I saw Dad calling everybody to the watermelon patch with hundreds of watermelons. Everyone picked one, which was great. The heart was the best part as it was tastier. We gorged ourselves. We'd never eaten so much watermelon.

There was no way we could continue pulling cotton, so soon after, we went home. It was late, and the watermelons were an unexpected reward. We had a wonderful time and were happy; we took some watermelons home to Mom. Things like that kept us going, and they included getting some candy and sodas when we stopped for gas.

17

CHAPTER

Mother

"Pictured here is my mom with 7 of the 9 kids when she came back to the United States in 1944. Note the official seal on the bottom right-hand corner."

M y mother was named Paullina Ybarra. She was born in a little town in South Texas just ten miles from the Mexican border. She never attended school; her parents were old-fashioned and did not believe in schooling their children. She worked cleaning houses, cooking, or in the fields. She never complained. So what if she did not know how to read or write? In those days, most people were not schooled. She also had a great singing voice, and could whistle many songs. Mom had given birth to thirteen kids. She was a powerful woman.

My dad had returned to the United States in 1943 with the two oldest sons to work in the fields to make enough money to bring the whole family from Mexico. My mom came to the United States in 1944 with the other seven children.

On my mother's side of the family there were many aunts, uncles, and cousins who were all hard-working and proud mileros who lived in Mission, Texas.They had picked cotton for many years, and our family initially picked with them.

One warm day, I saw mom pick cotton for the first and only time. I developed a deeper admiration for her and found out she was one hell of a cotton picker.

Let me back up a little bit. That time we traveled about twenty miles to the middle of nowhere looking for the house we were to live in while we picked cotton for the farmer. Manuel, an old man with us, was desperate for Dad to stop the truck because he needed to go to the bathroom. Dad told him to wait; we were close to the home we were supposed to live in.

When the truck stopped, the old man rushed to an outhouse beside the house but quickly rushed out. His pants were halfway down, and his face was pale white. "A snake!" He seemed to be running on air. Everyone laughed. Dad and Benito went to the outhouse and killed the snake. The old man had been lucky.

When Mom went to the back of the house to pee, she stooped down and saw another snake. She screamed, and Dad and Benito ran over and killed it. Well, by the time we settled in the old house, they had killed four snakes. So many snakes! But the danger did not scare me as long I was not next to one. We killed them in the fields when they rattled; we had to protect ourselves. When the weather turned cold, they went into hibernation in holes or caves.

That house was in bad condition—no electricity or running water—but we cleaned the place. Eighteen people slept in three rooms; the fourth was the kitchen. Some of my brothers slept in the car or the truck under lots of blankets.

We all went to bed early because the next day would be a big cotton picking day. The cool thing was that the cotton field was right next to the house, so we could walk to it. Mom and my oldest sister were up by five to make us breakfast, and we got to the fields around seven. We started picking slowly, but we picked up the pace as it got warmer. Around ten, I saw my mom coming from the house with a sack on her shoulder. When she started picking cotton, I could not take my eyes off her. I was exited; that was a very special event for me.

Dad came over and said, "Okay, your mother is picking cotton. When she's done, she'll give her sacks to the first member of the family who gets to her." We were happy about that. I claimed one of her sacks, which weighed about eighty pounds, and one of my sisters claimed the other, which weighed about seventy pounds.

Mother and my oldest sister left to prepare lunch for us. At about twelve, we went back to eat a hot lunch, a rare occasion. Mom always packed lunch for us when the fields we picked were far away, but this one was right next to the house, which was great. We all sat down to eat. I told Mom I had claimed one of her sacks, and she said that after she cleaned up, she would pick more cotton. When she came out again, I could not stop watching her. Dad used to tell us that she was a great picker when she was young. Two hours later, she went back to prepare dinner for us. She had great stamina. She helped clean the house and made sure everyone had a place to sleep. She set the table for dinner and cooked it. She would get up early to make breakfast, and then she would pick up to three hundred pounds of cotton.

My only regret was never having picked cotton beside her. I wanted to feel her warmth and talk to her as we picked. I missed that, but she implanted in me a sense of pride, passion, and a desire to work hard. That was the first and last time I saw her pick cotton, but that was enough for me. She was remarkable and my hero. She reinforced our family's values and inspired us all.

My older brothers had picked with her, and I thought that must have been exciting. I imagined racing her not to beat her but to stay up with her all day just to be around her and feel her warmth and power and hear her sing.

One time my mom came to me and said, "Son, since you have two jackets and two dress pants, I want you to pick one of each. Pick your favorite ones and the other I will give to your cousin because he is the same size as you. He needs clothing." Well I went and picked the ones I wanted and gave the others to my mom. She gave them to her sister, for her son. That was my mom - always thinking of others. She was so understanding, she knew I would understand. Why did I have to give up some of my clothing ~ this was family too. She was always right. Besides, she would buy me more clothing. And this was a lesson for me too ~ giving was very important.

We got our fortitude from my mother. Though she did not know how to write, read, or speak English, she managed to raise a large family. She and my dad were the heads of our family. She loved us and taught me many important life lessons.

18

CHAPTER

Dangerous Fields

My sister Olga was picking in front of me one warm day. Odilia, Otilia, and Olivia, my other sisters, were picking to my right, and my oldest brother was behind us. Olga called out, "Olivia! Come here and look at this rabbit!"

The rabbit was not moving. Something was wrong with it because rabbits always ran away when people got near them, but this one did not seem frightened. My oldest brother told us not to move. He came running with a cotton branch and saw the rabbit. We were wondering if he would kill it, which we didn't want him to do. "Shut up," he told us. We thought he was going nuts. He pounded on the ground near the rabbit, and then he bent over and picked up a very big but dead rattlesnake. We were in shock and speechless. If Olga had not seen the rabbit, the snake would have bitten her or one of us, and the hospital was far away. We all went back to picking cotton. Wow! My brother had risked his life for us; he had fearlessly protected his brothers and sisters.

My brother said that the snake had probably bitten the rabbit and had been waiting for it to die so he could eat it. He told us be more careful next time we saw rabbits acting strangely like that one. We were all in shock. I do not know if anyone thanked him, but we were very thankful. Snakes were a danger in the fields, so we had to be observant of our surroundings, but that was difficult when picking cotton; our minds had to be clear if we wanted to be good cotton pickers. Worrying about snakes slowed us down.

I wondered if I would have been able to kill that snake and thought, *No way, Jose— not in a million years.* My legs shook as I looked at the dead snake. *Maybe when I got older.* My big brother was our hero; he had not feared the danger he faced to protect us. I learned from him that day what to do in that situation to protect my sisters.

19

CHAPTER

Family

My oldest brother, Felix, was a hard-working milero. A few years later, he married a woman from Mexico after he had saved enough money. Their wedding in her town in Mexico was a big affair. He had someone film the wedding, and the event was mentioned in the newspapers.

After their honeymoon, they met us in a small town in Texas. He put his wife to picking cotton. She was a college graduate used to working in offices; she could type a hundred words a minute, but there she was picking cotton. Our family felt badly for her; it was hot, and she got blisters on her hands. It was too much for her. After two weeks, she started helping Mom to cook.

She was a great storyteller. At night, we sat close to her and listened to her wonderful fantasy stories; she had a way with words, and she became a big part of our family.

I had two other sisters-in-law who picked cotton with us. One was married to my brother Ruben, and she was a very good picker. The other married my brother Javier. After he was drafted, she came with our family on some trips to pick cotton. She had never picked before, but she became very good at it.

20

Growing Pains

My dad got back from seeing the cotton field we would be picking the following day and told me, "Son, tomorrow, we are picking in a great cotton field. I've never seen a better one." Dad was working on my mind; he was a great motivator, and he got me pumped up. I could not wait for the next day.

The following day, we got to the new cotton field. What a field! The cotton rows were full of cotton, and it was great. We all picked, and our sacks quickly became heavy. We were working on high energy because we knew it would be a great day for everyone. My first sack weighed 95 pounds—very good. Dad would park in front of the cotton rows and then walk with us. He counted his steps until he told us at one point to start picking. We would pick the row and end up back at the truck to weigh what we had picked.

We were picking so much cotton; we were picking two rows at a time, and I knew that I could not pick the whole two rows all the way back to the truck because I was picking too much. I took my sack to the truck and weighed it—120 pounds. I went back and finished the two rows before starting more rows.

Everything was going fine, but then I started slowing down, losing energy. I was not feeling sick, just weird and weak. Something was holding me back and making me wobbly. I took a rest on my sack and wondered what was going on. My sisters passed me and asked if I was okay. I told them I was just feel a little sick, and they went on picking. I wondered what was going on. This had never happened before to me. I would get up and

51

pick, but I would quickly feel weak and exhausted and had to stop again. My energy had vanished. I told my dad, and he said, "Just try your best, son. Don't worry. It's just the flu."

The whole day, I was behind the other pickers. I ended up picking 500 pounds of cotton while my sisters picked over 1,000 pounds. That day, everybody beat me. The nine-and eleven-year-old sons of one man picked more cotton than I had, and he had picked over 1,000 pounds. An old man named Manuel, who had only three fingers on his right hand, picked over 400 pounds, a lot for him.

I was not happy for having missed a great opportunity that day. I told the family I would make it up the next day, and I was feeling great the next day, but we started picking a new field that was not as good as the previous one. Cotton fields like the previous day's field came only occasionally; they were usually reserved for cotton machines.

My dad told me that I was experiencing growing pains, that my body was changing and I was reaching manhood. I did not understand that, but I guessed he was right. Benito called our parents the golden ones, and we had incredible respect and love for them. Our parents never had to push us to work hard; we knew our responsibilities and were unaffected by hard work. We got power and strength to pick from the encouragement and acknowledgment we got from our parents and the rest of the family; that took us to a higher level. We took pride in what we did though we did not know how long it would be our plight. We were not alone; thousands of other Mexican families were doing the same work to support and better themselves each year. We were all in a fight for survival; that drove us to become exceptional cotton pickers.

21
CHAPTER

The Twins

Olivia and Odilia were my twin sisters, and they were great cotton pickers.

One Saturday, I was sitting outside the house, which was across from the cotton gin. A brown car kept passing by. At first, I did not pay any attention to it, but the car with four Mexicans in it kept passing by. Finally, it stopped in front of the house. The driver got out and called me over, so I went over. He asked me, "Is your father's name Martiniano Chapa?" I said yes. He said, "My name is Dan. Can I speak to him?"

I went inside and told my dad some men wanted to speak with him. Dad talked to Dan for a while and invited him in. They came in and sat. Dan wanted my dad's permission to court Olivia.

The next day, Dan and his family—eight people in total—joined us in the cotton fields. Dan had told my dad that he was a milero. Dan raced Olivia that day—a challenge, a race between a man and a woman, and the whole family was watching. They went at it the whole day. All our family members were rooting for her. They went back and forth; he was trying so hard to impress the family. He thought our sister was going to lie down, but she was very skillful at picking cotton; she was a milera, so he had to pick over 1,000 pounds of cotton. He picked 1,007 pounds very good, but not great—my sister picked 1,037 pounds.

After that day, there was no more racing between them, and they never picked a thousand pound again. But they picked at a good pace; Dan would empty her sack every time they weighed their sacks; love was in the air. He was very lucky to get my sister because there was another man after her. This guy was a very handsome, tall Anglo. The first time I noticed him was at a gas station; he kept looking at my sister but not saying anything. My family and I realized he liked her.

Weeks later, Benito, Dan, and I were in the pool hall in Wellington, Texas, a town about twenty minutes from Quail, Texas, a tiny town near where we were picking. The guy asked if Olivia was our sister, and Benito told him she was. Dan came over and told him she was getting married soon, which shocked the guy, who did not know she had a boyfriend. Dan told him to stay away from her, and the guy said he would. I never saw him again. If I had been Olivia, I would have married him because he was well off, but she chose Dan.

Odilia was a great cotton picker; there was no woman like her, and most men could not beat her. She could put over a hundred pounds of cotton on her shoulder, carry it fifty feet, weight it, and empty the sack into the trailer repeatedly. It was demanding work day after day, month after month, but it was our trade, and we became proficient at it. We needed to earn enough to last us through March, and we were a big family.

Roman, one of my brothers, was a boxer, and it seemed that the whole family became boxers. I got good at it at a young age. Sometimes, Benito would take me and the boxing gloves on his bicycle, and he would find someone for me to fight. He would put my gloves on me and pick a boy to box with me. There was no contest; in a matter of seconds, I would beat other boys.

Well, one night, Odilia was playing around with the gloves and told me, "I can beat you. You want to box me? Put on the gloves." My sister was huge compared to me, but I said to myself, *You're going down.* I started well, but she was too big. My punches were bouncing off her, but hers were punishment for me. She was beating me up no contest, but then my chance to escape her beating came. She hit me hard, and my head hit a bed rail. I cried and pretended I was hurt, and my mother heard me. I told her what had happened, and she went after my big sister with a broom. After that, no more fighting with my sisters, just boys my own size.

Odilia was always singing, but she never finished her songs. I asked her why that was, and she said, "Stupid! If I knew the whole songs, I would sing them!" Ask a stupid question, get a stupid answer. I must have gotten stupid by the beating she had given me, and she must have gotten stupid from the beating Mom had given her. I ended up madder at her but perhaps a little less stupid.

One day, Odilia was at the kitchen table; on it was a plate with three jalapeño peppers. I dared her to eat a whole one without water, and she dared me to do the same. We bet a dollar. "You go first," I said. "No, you go first," she said. She loved jalapeños, but I did not; they were too hot for me. I grabbed one by its stem and pretended to put it in my mouth. I made faces as if I were in pain for a few minutes. She looked at me and was feeling sorry for me. I told her it was her turn, so she reached for a small one. I told her to eat a bigger one, and she did. She went through hell and was twisting all around. I was enjoying it. Her face was all red. I put my hidden pepper on the table and said, "Look, Odilia! I never ate mine!" She was mad; I raced out the door, and she chased me. I ran to my friend Lupe's house laughing all the way. I had gotten back at her for calling me stupid in the cotton fields.

22

People and Rattlesnakes

We were back on the road again picking cotton and would be doing that for the next four or five months. One week, I picked over 3,000 pounds of cotton and earned $60 for my family, and it was a great week for the others in my family.

We always went to town on Saturdays and spent the day eating, going to the movies, shopping, sightseeing, and meeting other Mexican families. This would be a very special day for me; I was rewarding myself, and I was full of confidence. I wanted to get a haircut, and I wanted an Anglo man to do it. I wanted to find out why I mistrusted Anglos and why they felt better than Mexicans. I was stepping out of my comfort zone. Dad had always cut my hair, but I wanted to get one in town on my own to experience walking into a barbershop, sitting in the chair, and asking the barber for a haircut. I was excited. I was winning my battle against stuttering too and was feeling great.

We all took showers on Saturday mornings. We always had buckets on the stove. We would take turns going outside to shower with a small cup and some soap after we undressed. It took a few hours before everyone was finished, but we finally got into the truck and headed to town in our best clothes. Dad would park behind the grocery store, and most of us went our own way, I went with Mom and Dad to a fried chicken lunch they paid for; we got a whole fried chicken for $1, what we got for picking fifty pounds of cotton.

After lunch, I got my allowance, $5, and went to find a barbershop. I saw one across the street. I looked inside and saw a man getting up from a chair and another man getting a haircut. I went inside feeling a bit fearful, but I sat in the empty chair, which felt nice. The barber was talking with the man; they were having fun, laughing. I felt good and relaxed and thought it was a nice place. The barber turned to me and asked, "What do you want?" I said, "I need a haircut," with a big smile. He said, "I won't give you one. Didn't you read the sign outside?" I told him no, I hadn't. He got angry. His face was red. He told me to follow him outside. I did, and I saw the sign. "If you cannot read," he said, "it says no Mexicans or dogs allowed. So get the hell out and don't come back!"

I was in shock, dumbfounded; I froze. I could not speak. The only words coming out were "ta-ta-ta-ta," so I walked away. My big smile was gone. My feelings of embarrassment were unbelievable, terrible. A pain built up in me. He never hit me, but his words were like punches that hurt horribly. I had felt great one minute and then terrible the next. I had been caught unprepared. I had not seen the sign. *Am I dreaming? No, this is really happening.*

Crying was my only defense. I heard the men laughing, and that hurt. They were having fun at my expense. I can still hear their laughter. I walked to an abandoned building crying and sobbing. That had never happen to me before. I was confused and had no one to turn to for help and comfort. I felt wounded. I could not think straight or see with so many tears rushing down. I had made a terrible mistake of leaving my safe surroundings and was paying for that dearly. I did not understand why those men were so cruel; I had just wanted a haircut, my first one at a barber's. *How dare those men be so mean!*

I would trust no Anglo barber again. I felt unwanted. In so many places, we were tolerated because farmers needed their cotton picked. This was their place, their town, but for us, it was just a stopover before another town and other people. I had learned big lessons—know your place, always be careful and stay with your own kind. That barber and his sign will stick with me forever.

We Mexicans were considered good only for picking their cotton; otherwise, we were worthless, undesirable, ugly. They could not wait for the picking season to be over and for us to leave. I stopped crying and walked to the truck trying to make sense of what had happened.

I walked to a grocery store and checked for any signs, but I did not see any. *Here, Mexicans are allowed.* I went in and bought a coconut. I went back to the truck and smashed the coconut on the ground until it broke open. I started to eat it. I could not tell anyone in my family about what had happened, but I knew it had scarred my heart and mind permanently.

Only good things happened in my make-believe world; there, all my dreams came true. I knew my make-believe world was just that ~ make-believe ~ but it was my security blanket, the only one I had. I needed to heal my wounds and pains and build my hopes back up. I loved to pick cotton; I just had to be more careful, more watchful. *I learned that some people were rattlesnakes who would not bother warning you before they struck you.*

I had wanted to come out of my shell, but their rudeness sent me back in. My immaturity was no match for those men, but I knew that in few weeks, we would move to another town. Those men would not be there, but I knew they and their laughter would be in my mind for years to come. In some ways, I blamed myself for not seeing the sign. I realized I had to be more aware of my surroundings because I could not change the fact that I was Mexican. I had been born in Texas and was a Mexican American, but hateful people thought I was just Mexican, someone ugly, miserable, and unwanted.

Mom told us a story that happened years before I was born. The family was traveling at night. Around two in the morning, my dad was hungry, so he stopped at a restaurant. He asked my mother if she wanted anything, and she said yes, a hamburger with cheese. Dad told her okay and went in; he sat at the counter and was eating his meal. Ruben and Israel woke up and asked Mom where Dad was. She told them he was in the restaurant, so they went to join him. The waitress saw them and went straight at them. "You're Mexicans. You're not allowed here!" They told her that Dad was their father, so she told him, "You have to leave too!" The three left.

Dad was angry. Mom asked him if something was wrong. "Yes," he said. "Your sons. We were thrown out the restaurant because of your sons."

"What you mean is our sons?" Mom asked.

"If it weren't for them coming in, I would have finished eating and would have gotten you a hamburger."

"That's okay," she told him. "Let's find somewhere that will serve us."

Dad did not look Mexican; he had a white-reddish complexion and spoke very good English; he could fool Anglos, but my brothers could not; their black hair made them look Mexican. I was beginning to understand why many times we ate on the side of the road and went to the bathroom outdoors.

Another time, Dad went to the cotton gin to weigh his trailer of cotton. When he went into the office, he saw some Mexicans gathered in front and told them good morning in Spanish. He opened the door, and one Mexican told him he could not go in there; only Americans could. "I was born in North America, so I can go in," he said with a smile. He went in and talked with some cotton growers. One of the Mexicans told the others, "That son of a bitch is more Mexican than we are. Why don't they run him out?"

Daddy was good with words, a likable person, and he had a lot of confidence. He always dressed well, wore boots and a hat, and had had some schooling in Mexico. His smile was big. When he came out, the Mexicans asked him why the gringos had not chased him out. "Well, maybe because I look like them," he replied.

23 CHAPTER

Tragedies

We heard of a terrible family tragedy. It happened to my little cousin. The family was picking cotton. When they were about to depart the field, my little cousin could not be found. They looked all over for him, yelling and calling his name.

After a while everybody got into the truck and they started driving down the cotton rows looking for him. There were hundreds of empty cotton rows. As the truck was moving, there was a bump. By the time my uncle stopped the truck, my cousin had been run over by the first and second back wheels. He was crushed and was dead. He had fallen asleep in an empty cotton row. Our family felt their pain. What a terrible tragedy ~ what away to lose a family member.

We lost another cousin. This one was while traveling to another town. The families were hungry, so they stopped in a restaurant to buy some hamburgers. They were sent to the side of the building where there was a window and they got served there. Since they were Mexicans, they could not go inside the restaurant and eat like normal people. Mexicans were not allowed. So, they went to the side window and ordered 20 burgers and left. They ate while they were traveling. Soon afterwards one of my cousins got very sick. He was rushed to the hospital, but he did not make it. Many members of the families thought that he had be poisoned by someone in the restaurant putting poison in the burger. My sister, Odilia, said that she had seen our cousin laying down on the back of the truck floor dead. Everyone was sad and crying.

Weeks after the death, while picking cotton, his father would cry out,

"Why did my son have to die? Why?" With tears running down his face, he would keep saying, "Why did my son have to be the one to die?" He was never the same after that tragedy. He was a broken man.

My dad told us about many other stories of the tragedies that happened. He wanted us to be aware of the many dangers out there. As we were getting older there were lessons that we needed to learn. He wanted us to be aware of the dangers out there in the towns, not just in the cotton fields. At least picking cotton you could hear the sound of a rattlesnake with its rattling noise warning you to not come any closer. Here you had a chance. But when someone poisons your burger, there was no warning or any chance to survive. There was no way to go to the police ~ who would believe cotton pickers passing through their town and a Mexican? So, nobody got punished for this crime.

Another time dad told us a story that had happened to this man's family. In the middle of the winter, after the cotton season had ended they wanted to get home so they were traveling at night, rushing back to their house. The three children were riding in the back of the truck. The man would stop now and then to check on them. They would complain, "Daddy it's cold. We cannot stand it."

Their dad told them, "Do not worry, pretty soon we will be home and you can sleep in your warm beds." Finally, they got home. When he went to the back of the truck to tell the children they were home, he found all of them dead. They had died because of the bitter cold.

There was an incident that took place late one afternoon as it was getting dark. We were in town shopping and having fun. Then dad called us quickly back to the truck. He said we were leaving because we were in danger. Some of the city men were after our girls. We went rushing back to the truck, got in quickly, and started driving home fast. Some family members had gone ahead with some of the girls to try and keep them safe. It was dark and we were going fast. I did not really know what was happening.

My dad was driving fast, not knowing if somebody was following us. Any car behind us could be persons that would harm us. I was young and feeling scared. One minute we were in town having fun and now we were fleeing. What did someone see that was a danger to the family?

After traveling for about 20 minutes we got to our house. As we were pulling up my brothers and other workers were outside the house in a line. The headlights of the truck was shining on them. I could see that some of my brothers had rifles and some had bats. The truck stopped and we rushed inside the house. I was too young to be outside with my brothers so I ran to the nearest window because I wanted to see what was going to happen. It was dark but then we saw some lights from two cars coming. They came close but did not stop once they saw all the men outside. They were out-gunned and out-numbered. They drove by very slowly and then quickly drove away.

I never found out what really started this chase. I just heard that some men were after our sisters. I was very proud of all our camp, standing outside and not fearing for their safety. They were right there ready for a fight. They would defend us at any cost. It felt good. I was undaunted by the chase because I knew we had the protection from all of our camp.

24

============================== CHAPTER

Braceros

N ew workers from Mexico called braceros had been coming to the
States ever since World War II to pick cotton in Texas and many
Southern states because they were needed for that.

My dad asked me if I wanted to see some of these people arriving from
Mexico to pick cotton, and I said yes. They numbered about two hundred.
They came in all shapes and heights. Some were dark-complexioned while
many were very white with blue and green eyes and looked very Anglo.

Benito, Ruben, and Javier were all given fifty men each; their job was
to take them to and from work and sometimes to the grocery store to
buy food. All the workers were divided into groups, counted, and driven
to work in trucks like animals. They needed the money to send to their
families in Mexico. Most had never pick cotton, and some had never even
seen a cotton field before. I was only thirteen then, but I knew how to pick
cotton very well. They were no match for me.

Two weeks later, I asked my brothers how their workers were doing,
and they said that some were doing well while others were just average
pickers. They said they all worked hard but were still learning, and it was
not easy for them. Benito said that the braceros were good people; they
were in a new world doing new things. He said they could not read or write
Spanish and knew no English.

"Just last night," Benito said, "when they were in their lodging, some
invited me to share their dinner. I asked them what they were eating. They
showed me cans of food with pictures of dogs on them. I told them they
were eating dog food, and they said no way could it be dog food because

it tasted so good. They said, 'You mean these crazy gringos feed this food to their dogs? They're crazy!' I told them that cans with pictures of dogs on them contained dog food, and one of them said, 'The next time I want good meat, that's what I'll buy,' and I just laughed."

One Wednesday, the family had just finished a cotton field at around three, so instead of going to a new field, we went home. Dad told me, "Let's go see Benito so we can see the new workers." We got there, and I saw some of the workers' sacks had straps that were too narrow and would cut into their shoulders eventually. And their sacks were not open; that would make it harder to fill and empty them. Other sacks were too short; they should have been at least twelve-foot sacks. Benito asked me to tell the workers how many pounds of cotton I had picked that day, and I told them seven hundred pounds. One man said, "I picked only three hundred pounds." Another said, "I picked only four hundred pounds. How does he pick so much at his age?" Benito said, "He's been picking cotton for many years, and he knows all the tricks."

They needed wires halfway around the mouths of their sacks to keep them open; that would make it easier for them to load the cotton in because they would not have to look back. Doing that took practice, but workers could master that as I had. And when the mouths of the sacks were full, they were supposed to grab the wire at both ends and shake the sack to drive the cotton deeper into the sack. My sack had an under layer to protect it from the ground as I dragged it. Those who had straps around their waists would make their legs sore. The straps went on their shoulders so the whole body could drag it. I thought that if they learned the tricks of the trade, they could begin picking another two or three hundred pounds a day, and in a year or two, some could become great cotton pickers. I wanted to teach them my tricks, but I was too young and very shy, and I stuttered.

We had been there for about forty minutes; most men had come in to weigh in and empty their sacks. Martin looked at six men going over and across empty cotton rows and beating cups with sticks making a lot of noise.

"What are they doing?" I asked Benito. "Just wait and see," he said.

I saw a jackrabbit jumping up and down and running toward us; one of the men caught it.

"Cool," I said.

"You bet," Benito said. "Sometimes, they catch three or four."

"Do they eat them?" I asked.

"Yes. They're very good. They will make jack rabbit soup for dinner tonight. When they chase the rabbits, sometimes, a rabbit would jump over one man, but there's always another behind him to catch the rabbit when it lands." We had always hunted rabbits with a rifle.

I had a wonderful time and learned some things. I felt sad for these men who were so far from their homes and families and did not know the language of this strange country. Just to buy food was difficult for them as they dealt with people who did not speak Spanish and were indifferent to them. I hoped and wished them the best. When I saw these men, I was seeing part of my culture. We were all Mexicans; the only difference was that I had been born in Texas.

If only I had been older, I could have taught them all my tricks. I was getting close to becoming a milero, and when I did, I would join the ranks of other mileros including most in my family. That was my goal.

25

CHAPTER

Traveling Men 1958

The year 1958 was a great working season for my family; we made good money. Dad told us that the manager of the cotton gin had offered him a job in Mexico. Ray Smith had rented a big farm there and wanted Dad to run it. Dad told him yes, so that meant the family stayed home in 1958. That year, Benito, Javier, and Ruben went to California; Israel was already there.

Ray was a very big and friendly man. Every time he came to the cotton fields where we were working, he would pick up Dad and give him a bear hug. He liked Dad very much. Ray was very playful and smiling all the time. He was a great man with a big heart; we all liked him very much.

The cotton season was ending, which meant I would start school for the year, but because I had always started school late in the school year, I was behind my age group though I was one of the tallest in my class.

Javier, a milero, was very muscular. Sometimes after picking cotton all day, he cramped up at night. He quit picking cotton to work in the cotton gin, and later, he worked in the oil fields. When he went to bars, he would challenge anyone to fight; he was a great fighter who never lost.

One time when work at the oil wells was slow and he was broke, he wanted to buy some beer for four guys sitting at a table talking and laughing. My brother was mad; he wanted to buy some beer for these guys to insult them, but he and his friend were broke. My brother raced home, got $2 from Mom and went back to the bar. He told the bartender, "Four beers for those assholes sitting over there."

The guys heard him and got up to fight. My brother and his friend left the bar still broke but smiling after beating the guys up. He had a reputation—no one messed with Javier Chapa. Since my last name was Chapa too, nobody messed with me. It was nice to have brothers with reputations. I was protected.

The following year, we were picking cotton in Wellington, Texas. One night, Dad took us to see a movie about life in the army. In one scene, the soldiers were complaining about always having to eat beans—beans, beans, and more beans. Our whole family was laughing so much that joyful tears were running down our faces. After working hard for many months, our bodies had taken a beating. We were weary and very tired. It had been a long year, but no one had complained. Seeing Dad and Mom enjoying the movie was wonderful. Dad was laughing as was Mom though she didn't understand English; she was enjoying her family laughing. It was as if Dad and Mom were hugging all their sons and daughters. That was a priceless time I did not want to see end—a magical night that reinforced our family's love for each other.

I stopped on our way out of the theater and looked back at the neon sign. I had been to the theater many times, but that was the most memorable and emotional time for me.

26

CHAPTER

Cigarettes and Drive-in Movies

One time, I was at the theater with two friends; we were smoking and having fun. Someone asked, "Is that you, Martin?" I turned and saw Benito, who said, "We'll talk when you get home."

I stopped smoking and got scared; I knew Benito would tell Javier, who would tell Dad. I got home, and Javier said, "I hear you've been smoking."

"Yes," I said.

"Where are the cigarettes?"

"Over here beside the house." I pulled out a brick, reached in, and grabbed the pack, which I showed to Javier.

"Well, Martin, we'll not tell Dad as long as you're buying the cigarettes."

"Okay, that's a deal."

"Little brother, tomorrow night, Javier and I are going to the drive-in. You want to come?"

"Yes!"

"How much money do you have?"

"One dollar."

"Benito has another dollar, and I have fifty cents. They charge fifty cents per person. This is what we'll do. Martin, you're going in the trunk. The back seat is removable. When we're inside, just push the seat over. Benito, I'll drop you off in the cotton fields at the back of the drive-in. I'll pay and get in. I'll park in the back. Benito, just climb the fence and get in the car." I was happy my brothers were taking me to the movies.

The following night, we drove to the drive-in and dropped off Benito.

I pulled the back seat down, got in the trunk, and pulled the back seat up but not all the way. I saw the cashier, who was beautiful. Once we were in, I climbed out of the trunk. We drove over to get Benito, parked close to the screen and watched the movie. During the intermission, we got popcorn and sodas. It was a nice night; I learned ways of seeing movies without having much money.

I quit smoking because my brothers were smoking all of my cigarettes, and it was costing me too much. Maybe it was their way of making me quit. If it was, it worked.

27

CHAPTER

The Old Truck

My brother Ruben had a *very* old truck. My sisters never wanted to ride in it with him because they were embarrassed to be seen by their friends. So, I rode with him most of the time.

One day after work we were driving back home from the cotton fields. He asked me to look in the mirror to see if there were police lights coming up behind us. Yes, there were. Then we could hear the siren. My brother pulled his truck to the side of the road and got out to speak with the police officer. After about ten minutes my brother got back in the truck. The police officer had given him five different tickets and a warning to get everything fixed on the truck within the next two weeks.

We continued to use the truck to drive back and forth to the cotton fields for work. We lost track of the number of days and one day when we were driving home, we spotted the same police officer who gave us the tickets. The truck was making a loud noise and as we got closer, the police officer turned around and saw us. He put his hand up, telling us to stop. My brother told me to wave at him, pretending that he was waving at us. We passed the police officer waving. Then Ruben stepped on the gas. The officer got in his car and came after us with his lights flashing. My brother knew there was no way his old truck could out run the officer so he decided to make a left turn. There was a mound with a canal going under it. Just as we were going over the mound, the truck stopped running. Right behind us were the flashing police lights. My brother got out of the truck with a big smile and asked the patrolman how he was doing. The patrolman asked my bother if he fixed the truck. My brother told him he needed more time.

He had a very big family and did not have the money to fix it. They talked back and forth. Finally, the patrolman left. Ruben got back in the truck with another five tickets. I think the officer felt sorry for him.

I asked my brother if he was going to fix the truck. He said no because the next week we were leaving to go pick in McCook, Texas which was in a different direction. Besides he did not have the money.

28
CHAPTER
Driving Lessons

When we were working in California, my dad was driving Ruben's old truck. We were on a dirt road in the middle of nowhere. It was just my dad and I in a truck full of melons. My dad started to give me driving lessons. He said, "Son, do you see that stop sign in front of us? That is like a patrolman telling us to stop." But as we got closer to the stop sign, dad did not make a complete stop. He said, "Well son, we will make the stop next time. Besides nobody is around."

A few minutes later dad asked me if those were flashing lights coming up behind us. They were and they were coming up fast. We stopped and got out of the truck. The patrolman asked my dad if he saw the stop sign. My dad said yes but that he did not see the officer. That made him mad. He gave my dad a ticket and a warning and told him he'd better make all the stops ahead and that he'd be following us. He followed us for many miles making sure my dad stopped at all the stop signs.

My dad then told me, "Son, that is why you have to make a complete stop. If not, you can see what happens."

Driving with my dad and my brother, Ruben, were exciting times. I learned so much about driving - the right and wrong ways!

29
CHAPTER

Vacationing with Dad

I remember another time when my dad was running a big ranch in Mexico. I got to spend the whole month with him. He rented a big horse for the month. I had a shotgun and a 22 rifle. There were two little pigs that I chased around. There was a big tractor and fantastic workers at the ranch. I had a wonderful time!

One Saturday when we were there Dad decided to go visit some friends in the city about twenty miles away from the ranch. After visiting his friend we went to a nearby cantina. As we got out of the truck dad gave me money to go see a movie. He handed me the truck keys and told me he'd be in the cantina.

The town was big. I went looking for the theater. First, I went site seeing, bought candy, and then I found the theater. I watched the movie eating popcorn and drinking a soda. After it was over I went to the truck and waited for dad. I got bored so I walked around the stores and barbershop listening to the people talking and joking. When it started getting dark I went back to the truck, got in, locked the doors, and fell asleep. Some hours later I woke up. It was late. All the stores were closed but the cantina was still open. An hour later my dad came out. I opened the door and he got in to drive us home.

After leaving the city my dad stopped the truck and said, "Ok, son, you're going to drive. There is no traffic here and it is just dirt road all the way to the ranch. You have to pass through three gates but you won't have to get out to open them. Kids will open the gates for you. You just need to throw them some coins and keep going. Also, another thing, when there is a Y in the road, keep to your left."

So, I started to drive. Dad fell asleep. I was the only one on the road. After many miles I got to the Y in the road. I said to myself, "Did he say to go to the left or to the right? I went to the right. As I was going down the road it didn't look like a road. It was very dark and the ground was limestone. Then the truck stopped. I started it again but then it stopped again and again. Finally, my dad woke up and asked what was going on. I told him I got lost and that the truck was not starting. He said we need to let the truck rest. He got out and went to sleep by a large rock.

In the moonlight I started to walk by the trees. I could hear water so I kept walking forward. As I got closer I realized that this was not a road. There was a cliff and water below. I started to cry. If the truck had not stopped, I would have killed both of us!

After an hour dad woke up and we started the truck. It worked. Dad said, "You drive. You're doing great, son! Let's turn around. The ranch is only another ten miles."

There we were again. I was driving and dad fell back to sleep. I started crying again saying to myself, "You're driving great." If only my dad knew ~ I almost got us killed! I got to the last gate and saw the kids running to open it. I threw them some coins and I could see the lights of the ranch. I went to my bed that night feeling tired and sleepy. As I laid there, tears were coming down my checks. Tears of joy! The feeling was wonderful! Somehow, I gotten us both back to the ranch safely. We were home.

30
CHAPTER

Becoming a Milero

Mileros were fantastic cotton pickers, and some became well respected and even legendary. You did not have to be a milero to be a good cotton picker, but being one was very special. They went to extremes and beyond.

For the stronger cotton pickers, there was always a desire to reach that milestone, that far-away marker, that invincible goal, the one-thousand-pound barrier – to become a milero. Getting there brought a feeling of pride, a joyful feeling that you had achieved greatness for that day and had accomplished something very special, something remarkable. The adrenaline you felt as you were getting closer to your goal was extreme, irresistible, and compelling. Sometimes, it was you and your mind talking to each other, your mind trying to convince your body that you were not exhausted, that you were too proud to stop.

When we talked to other families about cotton fields, stories of mileros always came up. Everyone knew great mileros—"This one was great, but there is another one I know …" My brother, Benito, had become a milero, the greatest milero I had ever seen, but our family was full of mileros, men and women including my mother.

Cotton fields were a big part of our lives due to our lack of education; we would not let the work defeat us. Trying to reach that thousand pound goal kept us going. We did not have a choice; we were following the example of older family members, following their steps, seeing them, picking hard. I idolized them as my heroes. Picking cotton was in our genes; we developed new ways of picking cotton, and we made innovations to our sacks. The more we picked, the more we forced ourselves to pick. If we could pick a thousand pounds in one day, how many more pounds could we pick the next day? Our parents' love, actions, and words gave us a reason to never give up, to realize we were doing something extraordinary. When you feel you do not belong, when you feel you are not wanted by the world outside the cotton fields, you push yourself in spite of the pain of hard work to achieve your goals. That takes inner strength and pride in what you are doing even though you are far from home. Cotton fields became a big part of my world, and I felt safe and free in the open space; I had hope for my life. On some special days, everything was right—good cotton field, nice weather, you were feeling great and full of energy, and you knew you were a proficient cotton picker. I had followed in the footsteps of my sisters, brothers, and mother. I wanted to be like them. It was brutal but not demoralizing work; we found purpose and fulfillment in it. Once you became a milero, you then wanted to become a greater milero; after achieving your dream of getting up that big hill, you looked forward to overcoming an even bigger hill and an even bigger one after that and feel even more joy and a greater sense of accomplishment. It was almost mythical, mystical, to make a dream come true. It gave you a feeling of invincibility; you were somebody, and you were achieving greatness in your mind, which continually gave you a reason to go forward and work as hard as you could. Pain did not matter or stop you, adrenaline kept you going and always reaching for that place of the mileros.

After I became a milero, picking over a thousand pounds became easier. I then worked hard to pick more. I wanted to remain a milero forever. That had been my childhood dream, and I achieved it. But it did not end. I wanted to pick more and more. The machines, however, were taking over. Families were leaving the fields. In 1964, I turned eighteen. I had little formal schooling, but I had learned a lot about life, and I was a hard worker who did not fear the future.

This way of life, which we would be leaving behind, had made me a stronger and harder worker, but I wondered if all the years I had spent pulling cotton had been all for nothing. No, they weren't. All those years picking cotton had allowed my family to survive and hope for a better future. And the fields had been my make-believe world. I was not afraid to express myself in them. I felt invulnerable there. That was a legacy I was taking with me into the rest of my life, where my and my family's picking skills were not needed.

31
CHAPTER

Contests

We often tried to see who could put the most cotton in his or her sack. The contests were a break from the normal, they wasted time, and thus money, but they were fun. Just like in the old days of gunslingers looking for the fastest gun, we mileros were always looking for other mileros and judging their abilities based on their height and movements. Right then and there, you knew if you could beat one or not.

We'd pick and once we got enough cotton at the top of the sack, we would shake it further down the sack by lifting it chest high and slamming it down to compress the cotton. Our sacks were fourteen feet long, so at times, we got in them and compressed the cotton with our feet. Our sacks ended up looking like hot dogs, and they would require two people to carry them to be weighed. The most cotton I put into a sack was 154 pounds, which was difficult to unload.

32
CHAPTER

Miseducation of Martin

S ome of my older brothers had left the cotton fields after many years and found jobs in other states. As my brothers and sisters married, they moved on to make their own lives. But many in the family continued picking cotton; we followed the lead of our parents. What carried my brothers and sisters and I was the devotion and trust we had for our parents, our pride and joy. We worked hard so we could survive the months with no work after we returned home.

My dad did not believe in taking aid from the government. My parents knew the owner of a grocery store named Lopez. We had an open account with him. He would help us any time we needed something. After we returned from our trips year after year, the first thing my dad did was pay our bill.

Some nights, I could not sleep. I would think about picking cotton. At school, I would daydream about that. Picking was a huge part of my life, my security blanket, my make-believe world when I was not in the fields. Maybe because I stuttered, I was very shy, self-conscious, and careful when I spoke. I never started conversations and being in one was painful. At times in school, the teacher would ask me to read something, and I would stutter. I loved school, but being asked to speak or read something aloud was stressful. I always sat in the back making no eye contact with the teacher. The fact that I missed school for many months any one year made me lag behind my classmates, and I had to repeat some years. I figured that my future was in the cotton fields, my own world where I was happy and could block out everything bad or hurtful. There, I could daydream and carry on a conversation with myself without stuttering. Elsewhere, I was always on guard and fearful because of my stuttering and my fear of others laughing at me for that. In my make-believe world, I was Superman.

When traveling, we were not allowed to eat in many restaurants and go into other places. Most people were nice, but many were not so nice. You could see it in their eyes, their mean looks. You heard it in their remarks. I was still young and trying to understand why we were not wanted, why we were disliked so much. *Why is there a hatred for our race? We came here to pick cotton, to make a living, so we could survive.* At times, my family members were told to leave stores. One brother would say he had been told to get out of a store, and another would say, "I was told they did not serve Mexicans." Some of my brothers had gotten into fights over that. Sometimes they won, and other times they lost.

I did not hate people I did not know, and our parents told us to tolerate and even respect cruel people—just walk away. They would say, "This is not our place. This is not Edinburg, our town. We're just passing through to get to another town."

The days we spent picking cotton together earned us enough money to buy nice clothes and gave us spending money. We had cars and trucks, and we owned a house in Edinburg that we would always return to after working throughout Texas—Lubbock, Abilene, Midland, Amarillo, Wellington, Quail, Calderon, Temple, Wheeler, Cameron, Tyler, Childress, and other places.

Not being able to go to school for many months and living in rundown houses was unavoidable if we wanted to make money. We sacrificed to survive; our schooling unfortunately came after that. We had to face very hot and very cold days, snakes, discrimination, and much more, but picking cotton was our livelihood.

33

CHAPTER

The Big Green Monster

"Martiniano, you're daydreaming again." I was. I was asking myself, *You want to race a cotton machine? Why not?* as I watched one. I had seen them many times but never this close. This powerful green machine could pick two rows of cotton at a time. This monster machine was the future. One day, this monster machine would replace us and leave us without work. Most farmers could not afford them, but soon, picking cotton by hand would be a thing of past and thousands and thousands of cotton pickers, mostly Mexicans, would be out of work.

The following day, I got my wish. A cotton machine was working in the same field. I started down the cotton row the green monster was coming up. It passed me. I waited until it turned around, then both of us were going downfield. As it got closer, I was ready. I started picking fast and then faster as the machine was coming up on my right. I was picking as fast as I could, but I did not have a chance. I was picking too fast, and most of cotton was going all over the place; not too much was going into my sack. In a matter of seconds, the cotton machine won the race.

I stood up to watch this beautiful, powerful, and fast machine. I laughed and admired it. I had some fun and excitement that day. In my make-believe world, I could beat that green monster. I would wonder, *Martin, what a wonderful time. How many young boys want to be in your shoes? Not one.* I loved my way of life, but I knew it was just a matter of time before it would end. We pickers would soon be the ghosts of the cotton fields.

However, until then, my family and I cherished this way of life. I watched my family picking cotton and developed my own style of picking. I knew when I was young that it would take years of picking to become as good as they were. I did become better, and I thought I would become a milero soon. I just needed more time.

The following year, we arrived in Quail, Texas, again. It was a small town, but we loved it. Quail was the last stop on our picking journey. That time, we had a storefront for living quarters across from a gas station. The store was abandoned but clean; we quickly made it livable. Jack, the owner of the gas station, sold us some food, sodas, and ice cream. He was always very nice to us. We loved it in Quail. Wellington was the town we went to for shopping, food, movies, and many other things. Behind our storefront was a cotton gin that operated twenty-four hours a day and made it hard for us to sleep.

On night we were awakened around 3:00 a.m. "Fire! Fire!" The tall grass behind our building had caught fire and was approaching us. Everybody ran outside. Fire engines came and put the fire out quickly. Most of us went back inside, but some of my brothers stayed out just in case the fire started again.

The problem was the cotton waste that came out of a long tube from the gin; wooden pieces created sparks as they traveled through the tube. The sparks had ignited the grass. That happened one other time when we were there. We did not sleep well until we cut all the tall grass around us. The following year, we returned to Quail and saw that the store had burned down. That was sad. It had been a nice place.

34

======= CHAPTER

What's a Fundraiser?

In school, I was the tallest in my class because I had been held back, but that was unavoidable because of our work. Jack, the owner of the gas station, once asked our Dad to take our family to a fundraiser at the school, where they would sell cakes people had baked. The following night, we all got ready; my sisters wore their Sunday best. I got dressed up too. Dad gave us ten dollars, and the girls had some money, and Mom gave us some more. We ended up with eighteen dollars, a lot of money. That was about what we would earn by picking a thousand pounds of cotton ~ a whole day's work!

We sat in bleachers in the school gym with many others. The fundraising started, people bid $10, $20, $30 on cakes. Some bids got up to as high as $150. *Man, these gringos are loco.* We just looked at each other with $18 in our pockets. When it ended, most people went home. There were some cakes remaining, but even those were selling for $8 or $10. We could not believe it. Some cakes had sold for $200, which represented one month of hard picking for us. But, I learned what a fundraiser was.

It was a friendly little town and the people there treated us well even if we looked out of place as we were the only Mexicans at the fundraiser. Yes, we looked out of place, but we were there to help with our donation, our hard-earned money. It was only $18, but to us, that was one hard day's work.

35
CHAPTER

Laws

Once, we were picking cotton in another town. We numbered about eighteen. As we worked, I saw some people ducking down. One crawled past me. Others seemed to just disappear. *What's going on here?* I wondered. I looked at the truck and saw Dad waving me over to the truck. Two police officers were talking with Dad. As I got closer, he asked me to get my little sister too, so I called out to Otilia, and we walked to Dad. He told us we were going home and would come back after 2:30 p.m.

The policemen were enforcing the child labor laws. Those younger than sixteen had to be in school when it was in session, so Dad took eight of us home and brought us back after school ended that day. The policemen warned Dad not to have any children picking cotton until after school was over for the day, and Dad agreed. The workers who were hiding were afraid the police would take them away and deport them to Mexico because they did not have green cards.

That went on for three more days—going to work after 2:30 p.m.—until Dad and the other families decided to move to another town. We needed the money.

36

CHAPTER

1,000 Pounds

One morning after a very good sleep—we went to bed around nine during the week—I woke up feeling great and sensing the day would be special. I washed my face and brushed my teeth outside the house because we did not have running water or a bathroom. We had a table and water outside for washing, and we used an outhouse. Mom had fixed eggs, bacon, beans, tortillas, and coffee. After the family ate, it was time to go. I could not wait to start working. I was excited about whatever was in store for me that day.

We drove about five miles to a place with a house, barn, and cotton fields that looked good. The cotton rows curved over the hilly landscape. As I picked, I looked around for someone to challenge. We numbered about ten workers, mostly family. The sun was bright, and I thought, *Great idea, Martiniano—challenge the sun. Mr. Sun, I'll race you. I bet I can pick a thousand pounds before you set.*

I started fast. I did not have time to waste. *This will be one hell of a race—picking hard all day, no breaks, no rest.* I told no one about my foolish race because they would think I was nuts, but I needed a challenge and was full of confidence. I filled my sack, and Dad helped me weigh it—seventy pounds. I dumped it into the trailer and headed for another row. I came back with sacks that weighed seventy-five pounds, then sixty pounds, and then seventy-five pounds. I was doing great and feeling great. I was going at a fast pace and was starting to feel fatigued, but I was waiting for my second wind. I knew I could last the whole day.

It was like playing a game I was very good at. I was having fun while

91

working hard to beat the sun and pick a thousand pounds for the first time and become a milero. I had gotten close other times, but I knew this time I would succeed. There was nothing stopping me. I skipped lunch. The last rows of cotton were very good. Not all rows had the same amount of cotton; some were better than others. I was picking two rows simultaneously. One sack I took back weighed more than usual; it was hard dragging that back. I told my dad I was getting a little tired. He helped me weigh it—ninety pounds. I emptied it and stopped for a little lunch and some water, and I rested for about fifteen minutes before getting back to work. I came back with eighty pounds. Olga, a milera, asked me why I was picking so fast.

I said, "I feel great! I want to pick a thousand pounds today."

"Good luck," she said. She had picked that much many times.

I came back to weigh my sack again, and Dad asked me, "Are you feeling okay?"

"Yes, just a little tired."

He said, "You've picked seven sacks so far—very good."

I said, "Dad, I need another pair of gloves." The sun was over me, not in the middle. It must have been around two. I had gotten my second wind and was feeling better. Working that hard had taken a toll on me, but I wanted to beat the sun. *I must pick faster.* I drank some water and picked another sack. At about three, I went back with a sack, ate some tortillas with beans, drank some water, and rested for fifteen minutes or so. *You can do it. You can do it!*

When racing, you try to block everything going around you. Some people like to sing while picking, others talk to each other while working—there is always something going on, so you block that out. I had no time to waste. I was on a mission, and I was going all out to beat the sun, which was in front of me. I did not have much time left. My body was hurting, and my legs were getting heavy, but I had challenged the sun and would win.

The sun got lower; it was getting orange. I thought I should not have taken those breaks. My sack was light. I had picked 960 pounds and needed 40 more. "Dad," I asked, "do you think I can pick forty more pounds?" He said, "Sure you can, son. Go for it. Pick that row over there. Someone didn't finish it."

I picked as fast as I could even though it was getting dark. Olga said, "Martin, it's getting late. Let's go home." I just kept on picking faster. Finally, I stopped. The race was over. It was too dark. The only light was coming from the stars.

I weighed my sack feeling defeated. I knew it was not forty pounds. It turned out to be thirty. Dad said, "You made it, son." I said, "No I didn't, Dad. I needed ten more pounds." I was devastated. "Son, you picked a thousand today. That was great." He was so happy for me, but I was not. I knew I had fallen short. I climbed up on the truck and lay in the cotton.

The truck was moving slowly because of all the cotton. The sky was filled with billions of stars—a bright night show, but it was not for me. I had challenged the sun and had lost. *What went wrong? I needed just ten more pounds.*

We got home, and my father told my mother I had picked over a thousand pounds. "Wow! That's great!" she said. But I was in anguish. "Son, sit and eat," Dad said. But I was not hungry. I was exhausted and sad. I did not deserve my parents' praise. I went to the next room where six of us slept on the wooden floor. I got two blankets and a pillow. I laid one blanket on the floor and covered myself with the other. On the radio, I heard the song "Are You Lonesome Tonight?" I was. I was also disappointed and hungry. But I slept well; a great singer put me to sleep. That song became one of my favorites.

I had lost a race nobody had known about. I had had a great day, but I had ended up ten pounds short. I would have made $20 that day if I had hit that mark, and that was a lot for a fourteen-year-old.

The next morning, I was very hungry. I devoured six eggs, bacon, beans, and many flour tortillas. We headed out for the fields to face the sun again. I had raced it the previous day not as a game but as a challenge. I wanted to develop the inner strength I needed to become a great picker. This was going to be my life, and I wanted to be among the best. I was disappointed with the outcome; nobody else knew what I was racing for. Any victories I achieved would enlighten my thoughts and drive me to overcome my defeats and make me grow as a person. I had to become a milero, a great milero.

As the years went by, I looked for ways to pick more and more cotton. I had to keep focused on the cotton fields, and I did so by racing myself, challenging myself to become a milero, the tenth in my family, and earn their praise. There was no rainbow at the other end, no pot of gold, but I desired to get there when I was young. I still had many years ahead of me, and I knew I could reach my goal with my parents' praise and encouragement.

Maybe it was a foolish dream of a foolish young man, but that dream was close to becoming reality. It was within reach—just a matter of weeks or even days before I joined my family on that plateau. I had gotten so close, and I knew achieving my dream would stick with me all my life. Yes, it would be very difficult to achieve that, but that did not matter. What else could I do but pick cotton?

I learned that every day, hour, minute, and second were important if I wanted to fulfill my dream of becoming a milero. That would not bring me riches, but I was not looking for them; I wanted the praise of my family more than anything, and *I wanted to continually inspire myself to achieve perfection as I defined it. If I did, I would be able to overcome anything.* My little world was different from the one where Mexicans were not wanted or respected; I faced demons in that world, who considered us outsiders though we were just trying to survive.

Picking eight hundred or nine hundred pounds was great, but picking a thousand pounds was fantastic. We pickers were not looking for much—just a better life, a better tomorrow for our families. We trained our bodies and minds to pick cotton as we were together helping each other achieve whatever we could. We would end a day picking cotton dirty, tired, and hungry, and go to a temporary place without bathrooms or showers. The next day, we would be at it again. This went on day after day, month after month, year after year. But we always had dreams and hopes for a better tomorrow.

37

CHAPTER

Working through Pain

We had to, and we did, go beyond the pain and fatigue we experienced in the fields. Our minds would tell our bodies that pain was simply pain. We overcame it by being passionate and zealous about our work and strove for our markers again and again. We loved the way of life that would be ours for years. Some escaped what they considered to be a prison, but others worked at it until they were too old to continue. Others worked until their deaths were their escape from it.

I was a foolish young man with a dream of becoming a great milero and earning my family's praise. That would make all my work in the fields worthwhile. I was becoming better at picking; I loved the sounds my sack would make as I dragged it behind me. I learned more about picking every day as I overcame my limitations, imperfections, and self-consciousness. Everyone in my family was trying to achieve the same goals and live good and then better lives. We endured hardships and disappointments, but we shared many good days and even great days. We trained our bodies to overcome our aches and pains so we could work the next day as hard as we ever worked if we wanted good things in life. We persevered.

We picked cotton with both hands and put it into our sacks thousands of times a day, millions of times a season. We submitted to this laborious effort starting in June in South Texas, when it was hot, and worked our way north to the panhandle, six hundred miles away, where it was cooler and sometimes very cold in December when we got there. We usually headed back home in January. That was our livelihood—working half a year so we could survive the other half. We had to deal with rain on occasion;

that would hinder our work, and being idle was not pleasant, but we took the bad with the good.

We pulled cotton with gloved hands; we would reach our fingers in the ripe pods that had split open and pluck it way down low. Some plants were short, but others were tall—many sizes. I picked cotton with my left hand, which gave it to my right hand to put in the sack. I kept my sack close to my right leg for that reason. I had to be careful when picking cotton close to the ground that no stalks poked my eyes. All these movements become instinctual after years of picking. The cotton fields were our schools in which we learned the value of efficiency.

We learned our lessons in that school because we needed to in order to survive. Our mission was never to surrender to this harsh way of making a living. We never lost our passion for it despite our aches and pains.

38

CHAPTER

The Art of Picking

Benito taught me to always make noise when I was picking so I would warn snakes before they warned me. Maybe that's why all my sisters sang while picking cotton. I could never sing, and I did not know any songs anyway. It was rare to come across snakes, but we did. Our tendency was to just concentrate on picking.

Some cotton plants have an overabundance of green leaves making it hard to see the cotton. The leaves fall after the first freeze of the year, the bolls open, and it is easy to pick. The fields seem all white. Cottonseeds sprout and grow into what looks like a thin tree with branches and tiny flowers that turn into bolls that grow to almost the size of eggs. Then they open like flowers do. The bolls have sharp, thorny points that you have to watch out for.

Cotton can be light or heavy due to the number of seeds it contains, and there are different varieties of cotton plants. Some can grow very tall, while others grow to only about twenty inches high. Our family consisted of very skilled cotton pickers who could pick any variety of cotton.

There are two ways to gather cotton. One is to simply pick out the fluffy cotton. The other is to pull the whole boll off, and that is the easier way. Pulling is where the money is. With pulling, you can pick over a thousand pounds of cotton in one day depending on the field. Using the pick method, the most you could pick is three hundred pounds of cotton in a day. Cotton machines strip all the cotton with bolls and leaves too, but there was lots of cotton left in the plants and on the ground. That's why many farmers prefer to use cotton pickers pulling by hand; they get a better grade of cotton, and it's cleaner. The cotton gin will separate the bolls and leaves from the cotton and seeds, and the cotton comes out fluffy and very white. Pulling by hand results in much cleaner cotton, but it does not matter which way is done. When the ginning is done, you cannot tell the difference between pulled and picked cotton.

One time, we were picking a field, and the cotton plants had lots of green leaves that made it tough to see the cotton and pick just that. We could not pick fast because we would grab leaves along with the cotton. When we emptied our sacks, we saw too many leaves mixed in with the cotton. We spent time removing the leaves, but still, the people at the cotton gin complained to Dad about the leaves. My dad told the owner of the field about this problem, and the owner told him he could solve the problem.

Within an hour, a small plane sprayed the fields ten rows at a time while we stood aside. The plants were wet and sticky, and they smelled. It was exciting seeing the plane come in low, spray some rows, go up, turn, and spray some more. A man on the ground was waving a flag to guide the pilot.

After the plane left, we went back to picking. We could still not see the cotton easily, and we were getting sticky with the spray on the plants. But the next day, we got back to the field and saw that all the leaves had turned brown and were wrinkled up, and we could easily see the white cotton. What a difference that made. Nobody complained. We went back to the picking. We did not know what chemical they used, but it worked, and everyone was happy.

Our goal was always to pick a thousand pounds. Some fields were good and allowed us to reach that mark, but others were bad, and we had to work harder. But each cotton boll you picked brought you closer to your goal; that's what kept us going and not becoming frustrated with this way of life. I was learning so much about life—what to do if I was confronted with a snake, many ways to pick cotton, how to weigh my sack, how to drive the trucks, how to act when in town, and trust nobody especially if they were not Mexicans. This was part of my schooling. I was learning about life, about how to survive. This way of life became my nourishment, my passion in spite of the pain of hard work.

39
CHAPTER

The Flu of Clarendon

Clarendon, Texas—how could I ever forget that place? In late 1958, only four of the 30 workers did not get sick. All the others were in bed with the flu. The fevers and the coughing went on for over two weeks. They were too weak to get up and eat. Javier got sick and ended up in the hospital.

Some people from a church would bring us two big pots of soup and a case of Coke. The coke went fast, but the soup took longer. In the beginning, we would not eat the soup, but after a week, we got used to the taste, and it was better. The church people were wonderful. They told us that people all over the country were catching the flu—it was an epidemic. We were bored not doing anything; we played cards and slept a lot. Once, we went into town, and it looked like a ghost town; there were no people. We got scared and went back to the house.

Finally, the workers got better one by one; they were getting up. Once, I tried cooking eggs and smoked up the whole kitchen. Benito rushed over and asked, "What are you burning?" I said, "Eggs." He asked, "Where's the oil? You need to cook them in oil!" I had not known that. He cooked some eggs for me.

After the third week, we all went back to picking but at a slow pace; we were all still weak. It took two days to get back to normal. A few weeks later, we headed back to Edinburg; we were done picking for the year. Going home was always a joyful time. There, we felt free to walk the streets without people staring at us and making bad remarks. We could put our guard down, and school was starting for us though we had missed many months. We were happy being back. Our bodies needed the rest. We knew the work would start again, but we were used to this way of life.

40
CHAPTER

Roman and Ruben

My brothers Roman and Ruben were in the military. Roman was in the air force, and Ruben was in the army. Our family was so proud of them. One time they both had leave at the same time. They came home to see family. The day they arrived, I was by the road beside the house waiting for them. I saw two buses coming from opposite directions. They passed each other and stopped about fifty feet from each other. Roman got off one, and Ruben got off the other—the timing was perfect. They were surprised to see each other as we were too. What a great day for the whole family to reunite with two members who were serving their country. They were able to stay for a week.

41
CHAPTER

Kennedy: 1960-1963

In 1960, the elections were going on. I stayed up until around five watching TV waiting for results of the race between Nixon and Kennedy. I was rooting for Kennedy. I did not know why, but I liked that man. There was something special about him, and I was so glad when he was declared the winner.

In November 1963 I will never forget what happened. It had been raining on and off, and we had not been able to pick cotton. We were supposed to pick the following morning, November 22, 1963. We got to the field around ten, a little late, but Dad had wanted to make sure the fields were dry before we started picking.

Hours later, Dad called us over to the truck. He told us Kennedy has been shot. He did not know why. We all got closer to the truck so we could listen to the news that saddened us—terrible news. Nobody was talking; we were just listening to the radio hoping and praying for good news, and then we went back to picking. But something was missing. Our energy was gone. Our minds were searching for answers. We were picking very slowly. The pain and shock were unbearable. Our bodies and minds were not up to it. We were worried we'd lose someone dear to us. We were hurting though I did not know why this man was important to us. We knew we had to pick, but we had no will to pick. Our hearts were broken.

Maybe he would have fixed the country and made it better. He had given us hope. Then Dad called us over. Our president had died. We were in shock. We could not believe our president was dead. Dad told us, "Let's go home. Stop picking. This is a way to pay our respects to our president."

That day affected the whole family, and we found out later that it had affected our whole country.

Later that year, we headed home. We were mentality fatigued. We had had a very good year picking cotton, but with the passing of our president, something was missing.

42
================= CHAPTER

California, 1963

In 1963 when the cotton season was over in Edinburg, Dad decided to travel to California to see Israel, my brother, who was overseeing a big plant there. So instead of following our regular route up to the panhandle, we went to California.

My brother Israel had a wonderful job there. He was the foreman at an alfalfa-processing plant. He had been the first great milero of my brothers and sisters, but I had never seen him pick cotton as I had been too young then. But I was told he was a great one, one of the first in our family to become a milero.

That year, we picked walnuts, apples, prunes, and other fruits. Housing there for fields workers was great. We lived in camps run by the state; they had running water, electricity, bathrooms, and showers for men and women.

We spent the first night in the camp. Dad said we were getting up early for work. I woke up early and heard people, but it was so early that I kept on sleeping and woke up around five. The camp was quiet. I went to take a shower, and there was nobody around. The place was empty; people had already left for work. California was new for us—it was not Texas. We got to the fields around six; that was late. The others had started much sooner because after eleven, the sun would be too hot; people had to stop working then.

These workers were excellent; they had it figured out. They went to bed early so they could get up by three and get to the fields before first light, work until noon, and get back to the camp. The great thing here was that we were paid daily and spent the rest of the day doing whatever we wanted to do. We had never seen housing like that before; they had everything we needed or wanted.

It was, however, hotter than Texas; it regularly reached over a hundred degrees, but I could take showers there daily. In Texas, we were lucky if we could take showers weekly.

We traveled by truck and cars, which became hard and boring. We traveled in the back of the truck and would stop just for gas, food, and restrooms. If we did not find restrooms, we did it in the woods.

After seeing my brother and his family and working for months in California, we left for the cotton fields of Wellington, Texas. We had picked cotton there for many years, and it was a great place ~ a second home for me.

<h1>43</h1>

<h2>CHAPTER</h2>

<h3>*Second Shot at School*</h3>

In 1961, when we came home from the cotton fields, I had just turned fifteen. I started school in January in the sixth grade, but two weeks later, they sent me to seventh grade. Those in my age group were in high school. I went to summer school and did great there. I needed one more year to get to high school, but I could not because my family needed me in the fields with them. I was too good of a cotton picker. Our family was getting smaller, and I was needed.

Dad signed me up for business school to learn accounting because he knew picking cotton was coming to an end. Most of the family was not picking any longer; they had gotten other jobs, so the following year, I stayed with Xavier and his wife to learn a trade—no more trips. The first two months of business school were good, but then I started to go to the pool hall more and school less. I could have learned a trade and had had a better life, but I had wasted my parents' money and had not earned what I could have in the fields. I could not face my family, so I decided to join the army.

I was sent to San Antonio and took some tests that I did not pass. I was disoriented. The bus trip back to Edinburg seemed to take forever. Everything was going wrong. I got home in the middle of the night. Xavier asked me, "Is that you, Martin?" I said yes. Before he asked any questions, I told him I had not passed my exam. He said, "In the morning, get ready for school."

My family arrived the following week; I told Mom that I had not gone to the business school, and she was not happy. My father told me that the reason they had sent me to school was for me to learn a trade. I started crying, and so did he. His words were hurting me though he did not mean them to. I was very embarrassed; I had no explanation for having done wrong.

I was waiting for him to hit me, but he was too proud. He forgave me. He said that if I did not want to go to school, I would work in the fields for the rest of my life. "Son, I did not want that for you. I wanted something better for you—a trade. But if you don't want that, you can work in the fields."

Therefore, I went to work in the fields with a new urgency. I was mad at myself for having let my family down. I had reached a low part in my life. I had done something out of character.

So, I worked in the fields picking, lettuce, tomatoes, onions, and cotton when the season stared in Edinburg, and then three months later, we traveled north picking our way to the panhandle as usual. Dad took us to New Mexico, where the cotton was better. They had been there the previous year, and it seemed the year would be a great one. I wanted to work hard for my family to repay the bad I had done to them. I went all out that year to regain their respect. I wanted to make it up to my parents; I wanted to pick cotton as I had never done before. The pressure was on me to excel.

44

CHAPTER

The Great Race—Benito and Me

"Benito circa 1964."

O ne night, the sky was bright—billions of stars were shining on us. I remembered the day I raced the sun. I was much older now, almost at my prime. I was a milero. I had mastered the art of pulling cotton. I was more mature, faster, and stronger than ever, ready for a race. I sensed there would be a great race the next day. The signs were in the sky. Benito had wanted a race, so I knew it was coming. I knew tomorrow would be a great day. The stars were shining on me.

I could not sleep. I was excited and waiting for morning to come. I had raced my brother many times in my make-believe world and had always won. Our race the next day would not be make-believe. We would be going to the extremes and into the unknown zone. This race would be more painful than any race before, and we would use everything we had learned in the cotton fields.

Morning came. We had breakfast. The cotton field was only a short distant away, and some of the cotton was right in our backyard. We got to the field, and Benito looked at me. He challenged me. He had challenged me in California picking walnuts, and what a race that was. We had gone after each other hard and fast. We each had two buckets we had to fill with walnuts and empty them into a big wooden box. A man there gave each of us a card with numbers from one to a hundred. Every time we came to empty the buckets, the man would punch the cards twice; that was how we got paid.

We were going fast, almost running. My brother would empty first, but I was right behind him time and time again. The man punching the cards was amazed at how fast we were filling the buckets hour after hour. Benito was always emptying his buckets ahead of me, but I was always right behind him. I could tell he was tiring; I could sense it, and that gave me more drive to stay right behind him until he gave up. I would not give up. I would beat my hero, my brother, the greatest cotton picker I had ever seen. But that day, we were picking walnuts, and I wanted to beat him.

We both picked a hundred buckets, received new cards, and went back to picking. I had my back to my brother. I felt a sharp pain in my right side. I looked back and realized my brother had hit me with a walnut. I saw the look in his eyes—he had given up. I lay there crying until the pain went away and then started picking again with joy and a big smile. I had won. I had defeated my brother, and I was so happy. He told me he was sorry. "That's okay," I said. I knew there would be others races in the cotton fields, and cotton was not as hard as a walnut if he threw any at me. What a demonstration we had given to all the people picking walnuts. They had never seen anyone pick so much and so fast. Those in charge told my dad, "You have great sons there."

Dad never had to push us to work hard. We knew what was expected of us and the circumstances we were in. Some years, we traveled thousands of miles to work; the whole family worked hard and tried to be the best. The day of our cotton-picking contest was going to be the greatest day in my life. I had worked all these years hoping for a day like this. I had never seen anybody pick better and more cotton than Benito. He had big hands, was over six feet tall, and weighed about 170. I was five foot ten, weighed about 100 pounds, and I had good hands and great endurance. I was coming of age. This would be a battle. Milero against milero—brother against brother. I felt untroubled by this challenge. I planned to race him just as I had raced him picking walnuts. I would stay just behind him. I wanted him to feel pressure. I would wait until he tired. That was when he would see I was not going to quit, that his little brother had grown into a great milero too. This would not be easy, but I would push him to the extremes. Maybe it would challenge my endurance. I knew that day would be a day of suffering, but I had prepared for this for many years.

It was a privilege racing Benito. I would not settle for second place. As we picked, I said to myself, *Martiniano, this going to be the longest and hardest day of your life. He will try many tactics on you, so watch out. He has more experience than you and many more years picking.* I was sure Benito considered our race payback time for our walnut contest in California.

He started fast right away and left me behind but not by much. I did not panic; it was going be a long day. I planned to stay close behind him. He was the first to weigh a sack—eighty pounds. I came to weigh mine not long after—seventy-five pounds. He was already five pounds ahead of me and was back to picking.

I walked fast to another cotton row and started to pick fast, but he was faster. I could not match his speed, but with time, five or six hours, who would be more tired? I put pressure on him. I had nothing to lose as his little brother while he had immense pressure; he had never lost a race, and to lose to his kid brother would tarnish his reputation. My chances were a long shot, but it would be a long day. He was ahead of me, but that was okay. We were both picking quickly. He wanted to drive me to the ground, but that would not happen.

Lunchtime came, a special treat. Dad had cooked a steer head the previous night. He had wrapped a head in canvas and put it in a hole he had dug. On top of that, he placed a large tin platter and built a fire on that. He buried everything, and it had been an oven overnight. Dad took care of it at night, and my mother took care of it in the morning.

I weighed and emptied my sack and asked Benito if he was stopping for lunch. He said he was not. I knew what was happening; he was trying to get way ahead of me while I had lunch. That was not fair, but I realized he was running scared.

After a great lunch, I went back to work, and I was full of energy. Soon, Benito would need food and would tire, but by then, he was over 150 pounds ahead of me. I was getting close to a thousand pounds, unheard of. We were going at a tremendous pace. It was my greatest day, but I was well behind my brother. Nonetheless, I had four hours left to pick. By two thirty, I sensed my brother was slowing down. *Martiniano, you're getting to him. He's hitting a wall.*

That day, picking cotton was effortless. I was not tiring at all. It was unreal. I was in a new zone and working with intense energy. I was breaking my record with every pound I picked. I had thought that would be impossible, but Benito and I were doing the impossible, reaching a point not many had ever reached. I was not tiring, but I knew Benito was. He had not eaten all day. I was not dreaming; this was a happening. I went faster and kept it up until three thirty. By then, we were next to the house, which was sixty feet away. Benito signaled he was coming in; he asked my dad to help him with his sack. Dad told him to just leave it there. My brother could not finish his row though there was only forty feet left. But he was done. Just like that, he stopped picking. He had no will or strength to continue. I watched him walk to the house and go inside. Dad was happy for him. He knew he had seen a show; one of the greatest cotton pickers was leaving the cotton fields maybe forever. My brother had picked over 1,500 pounds of cotton in less than a day.

I picked for another two hours—*Why stop?* By then, I had picked over 1,350 pounds, my best day. *Oh brother!* I had won. He had quit, but I knew that would be the easy way out for me. I had a decision to make. I could keep picking cotton and win. I looked at my Dad, who said, "Martiniano, if you want to, you can go home too." That decided the matter for me. I went home with a tremendous respect for Benito, who had shown lots of courage. I had driven him to the ground, but he had had his best day as a cotton picker, and by doing so, he had pulled me along to my greatest day too. I had reached a zone in which the hard work was refreshing. I had wanted to perform at the highest level, and I had done so. I was not tired. I could have picked more and beaten my brother. It would have been my last chance to defeat him, but I stopped too and went in.

What a day, what a great day racing my brother. This one was for the ages. I kept my composure, but inside, I was full of pride. Our family was a family of great mileros and mileras, and I had been the last one to reach that goal. I had learned all I knew about picking cotton from them. They taught me to work hard all day and then work the next day just as hard. We all knew this was a heartless way of making a living, but we were fighting for our survival. They were my teachers, my heroes, and I looked up to them all. They taught me to attack rather than just pick cotton. Dad carried in my sack too. I knew he was very proud of us; he had witnessed two sons at their best and was overwhelmed with pride.

I wondered whom Dad wanted to see win. I never asked him, but maybe he did not want one winner but two. Dad had been in the cotton fields for over twenty years. He had seen all of his sons and daughters pick cotton, and he was very proud of all the family.

Later, Benito told me that his right leg had been hurting so much that he could not take the pain any longer. I realized that even if I had beaten Benito, he was no longer the Benito I had wanted to beat. Let me explain.

At one time, Benito was in California working in irrigation fields. He was driving a tractor with a trailer of long irrigation pipes and two other workers. The road across the field was very bumpy; every time the tractor hit a bump, it would bounce high. Well, they hit a big bump, and the tractor tipped. The gearshift jammed into his stomach. The tractor did not fall completely over because it was still attached to the trailer; it kept moving. My brother was in incredible pain. The two workers were thrown to the ground unhurt, but they were in total panic. Benito told them to go for help. Somehow, he managed to turn the tractor off, but he was still pinned by the gearshift. Help finally came, and no one could believe my brother was still alive. It took many men to get him off the tractor; they took him to a hospital. My brother was screaming for them to cut his leg off; he could not stand the pain. That went on for days. He was only nineteen.

After a year in the hospital, he recovered, but his left leg was in a brace. He walked with a limp, and he could not move the toes of that foot. A few days after he got out of the hospital, he came home to Edinburg, where his girlfriend was.

I knew that on the day we had challenged each other, he was surprised at himself and maybe at me because at age eighteen, I had done what he had done at the same age. That day, he realized he was still the champ and had picked more cotton than ever before. Besides, he had proven the doctors wrong; they had told him he would never walk again. But even with a bad leg, he was still the greatest milero of his time. I knew that if Benito had not gotten hurt back then in California, he would have picked 2,000 pounds that day. We both won that day though he was twenty-four and I was eighteen. He had almost died five years earlier. What we did that day was astonishing and unbelievable. We had gone to the extreme, beyond what others had accomplished even with so much daylight left. Though few people outside our family would know of our great accomplishment, we would remember it for the rest of our lives.

That was our last year picking cotton, and we went out victorious. We felt we had beaten our adversary, the cotton fields, and that way of life. We had left our mark on the cotton fields that we would soon be sadly leaving. The cotton machines were taking over. They had gotten better, and more farmers were using them.

Four of my older brothers and two of my sisters were not pulling cotton any longer. Maybe they had seen no future in it. Times were changing. Some in our family were getting better jobs and better futures. Traveling so far for so many years had taken its toll; our parents were getting on in years. They had made these trips for over twenty years spending half the year away from home. It never made us rich, but they had raised a very large family this way. My other three sisters were going to Chicago the following year to work in factories. We had to support our parents, but I did not know what I would do.

I had inherited a fascination for cotton; I wanted to follow in my family's footsteps. I wanted to be like them. I had never imagined our way of life ending. It had taught me so much, and I was at peace with my way of life. It was my playground, my protection. Striving to become a milero kept me going; it gave me hope. It was my aspiration.

In the middle of nowhere, with just my family and some others picking cotton, I was living my dream. Maybe I had reached my goal too fast and at too early an age. Maybe I had been born in the wrong age. I had sacrificed so much pulling cotton, and I wanted to leave my mark on the cotton fields as they had on me.

Once I turned eighteen, things would change. There was a war going on. I realized I would be drafted. I would be called up to serve; that was my only hope for a better future. I realized I would not grow old in the cotton fields even if I wanted to.

At last, we had a small window, a chance to make a living doing something else. What we took from this way of life was our work ethic, discipline, and character. We had fulfilled our dreams even if they had been small dreams. We had achieved something important for us as a family and would carry it with us for the rest of our lives. I felt ready for the rest of my life. No matter what lay ahead for me, I had had the privilege of fulfilling a great dream I had had since I had been a young boy.

Maybe I would have to fight, but if I made it back, I would look for my future. The war was taking many of the young men. Our days in the fields were numbered. Mileros would be a thing of the past, but I would make sure their legacy, their compelling way of life, would be remembered.

Below is an insert from a letter my brother wrote me in 2018 recalling the tragedy. He passed away in 2019 and will always be remembered.

Below is a personal letter from my brother Benito before he died. He sent this to me detailing that horrific day he was crushed by the tractor.

My awful accident
August 7 1960

The men had taken the tractor off me.
That awful accident would leave cripple for the rest
of my life. Although at that moment I wasn't
aware of how serious my injury was.
I had asked the men that had taken me off that
Tractor's gear shift, to lay me down under the
Trailer that I had been pulling with the Tractor.
     I had been Pined between the Tractor and the
Iron box that was welted on the Trailer's hitch
with the Tractors gear shift deep inside my Stomach.
The bleeding hadn't stoped and was making me
very week, thats why I had asked the men to
lay me down under the Trailer, cause I was very
Sleepy, that the only thing I wanted to do was
to go to sleep. That beautiful serene sleepy
Sensation was so peaceful that I felt that I was
Floating in mid air.
     He were Black.
The man that were Black had told the men, Not to
lay me down, and don't let him go to sleep, saying
Cant y'all see that (He is dying.?)
I had Felted Thunder Bolt Stricken by the men that
were Black statement, That I was dying.
I didn't wanted to die, Not just yet, thats why I went
into a deep silent prayer. I wasn't scared that I
was dying, I was very sad that I wasn't going to be
     Able to send money to my Golden Couple No more
so they could make ends meet. I had been in
California For 3 months and I was making about
40 dollars a day I was very proud of my earning's
that I would send my Golden Couple more than 90% of it.

Since I was working every day of the month I needed very little For myself.

Besides my Loving heart always Felt very happy For my Golden couple Knowing that they would (Do With,) even iF I would (Do With out) something's.

Many a time's as I was growing up I saw our Wonder Ful Golden Couple our Loving Parents (Do With Out) so us their Loving children would (Do With), things, and even Food.

There was 3 months of Hardship For our Golden Couple From February through April, very Few jobs could be Found. I will Forever remember one of my most Sadest nights in my young tender loving heart I was about Ten year's old.

We the Chapa's we were a big Family, my saint mother had cooked a big Pot of Beans and had added a small portion of Ground Meat to give it a little meat Flavor. She Shouted come on Children the Food is ready. We all came into the Kitchen and Sat at our big table, again we the Chapa's were many mouths to be Fed, 9 brother's and 5 Sister's.

I could see our Saint mother's Loving glances Toward my (Mountain of a man) our Loving Father were Filled with immense joy, For her Loving husband was providing even in Hard Ship Times. Our Saint Mother had Served all of us and remained standing up, one of sister's had said come on mother sit and eat with us, she said No I'll eat later. She kept saying eat up There's more Where that came From, and she would serve us more Food. As soon as we had Finish eating Mother said okay Y'all get up and leave the Kitchen so I can clean up.

3

I had returned to the kitchen For a glass of
water and had surprised our saint mother

Wiping a thin layer of Beans off the bottom of
The big Pot, she had wipe it with a small piece of
Leftover Tortilla. When she had turn to face me
I could tell that I had surprised her. Right away
She said You know son that its a Sin to throw
good Food away. The instant I saw her wiping
the bottom of the Big Pot with that small piece of
Leftover tortilla, I knew there wasn't any good
Food Left, she had served it all to us her Loving
children, and that she was Hungry. Our Saint
mother had (Done Without) so her Loving children
would (Do With).
I can still recall that Night was very sad For
me I Felt my young tender Loving Heart heavy
with Immense sadness, For I knew that my
saint Mother had gone to bed with Hunger.
I remember asking God to help me get older Quick
So I could became The Fastest Cotton Picker in the
Chapa's Family. I wanted to help my Golden Couple
make ends meet, and to do that I had to be big and
Strong.
I knew Now how childdish I was to have
asked God to make me older Quicker. My only excuse
was that I was a mire child in his Fantasy world.
that things seemed easy to me especially Knowing
God would give me a helping hand.
Besides in my child world I didn't wanted my
Golden Couple to go to bed with Hunger.
And our Saint mother always told us her loving
children that if we would asked God to help.
That he would help us.

118

4

The years had passed, I had becomed the Fastest Cotton Picker in The Chapa's Family

I had become a hard worker like all my loving Siblings before and After me (But Now I was Dying And far away From my Golden Couple and most of my loving siblings, I knew I had to pray.

In my deep Silent Prayer I had asked God, Please God don't forsake me Now, Please help me live to see my Golden Couple and my loving Siblings even if its for the last time, Please God, Please, I wasn't imploring I was begging.

I wanted to tell my Golden Couple my loving parents that I was very sorry that I wasn't going to be able to help, no more. In my silent prayer I had included Virgen Mary, La Virgen de GuadaLupe, and my Lord to help me see my Love Ones one more Time. I musta been Delirious to have asked for such an impossible prayer to see all My Love ones, They were in Texas I was in California Two Thousand miles away.

Although I was 19 years old I didn't allowed, myself time for Romance besides The Girl of my dreams and my Hearts desires. wasn't in sight just yet. My Saint Mother was still my main Girl in my Loving Heart.

The four men were dumbfounded by the man in Black statement they were still carring me and wouldn't lay me down for fear of me dying on them. Until one that was helping carry me had said (EL hijo del Patron) Meaning (The son of the Boss) had arrived at the seen. I saw a brand New light Blue Ford pick up Truck come to a complete stop right beside us.

119

The Son of the Rancher dashed out of his
Pickup as soon as he saw me He started saying

Oh my God, Oh my God, Oh my God For the longest.
Him saying Oh my God For so many times had
convince me that Yes I was to die sooner that
I wanted. But since I still had that beautiful
Sleepy sensation dying wasn't bothering
me that much, I just wanted to go to sleep.
The Son of the Rancher dash back to his Pickup
Took his Two way Radio and said Dad I have a
Mortalley wounded boy I want you to call the
Hospital at (Los Baños) meaning (The Tubbs) a
Little Town that was about 30 Miles away.
Dad I also want you to call The Hiway Patrol
I need a Fast escord, I don't think The boy is going
to make it, I'll be on Farm road so and so. He got out
of his pickup Truck and told me we can't wait For
an Ambulance, I must take you to the Hospital right
Now. Then he asked me who do you want to ride
with you on the back of the Pickup, cause you can't
ride in the Front. You have to ride laying down
Maybe laying down you won't bleed that much.
I had pointed at the man that wore Black Suggesting
that he would ride with me in the Back of the Pickup
Truck. He jump onto the Back of the Truck and
set with his legs across the Truck' Box.
I was leyed with my head on his Laps he took off his
Black hat holding it chest high to shade my Face
From the Sun. As soon that the Truck started
Moving on that bumpy dirt road my Blood
was gashing out of my wide and deep wound.
The wound was very wide cause when I had Tiped
the Tractor on me I became Pin between the

Stirring wheel of the Tractor and A Iron box that was welted on the Trailors Hitch.

We would carry Elbow's and Valves in that Iron Box For the irrigation pipes that were about 30 Feet long. The Tractor had no key Hole I had connected the wires direct. When I had Tiped the Tractor on me the Tractor kept moving on it's back Tires. The Front tires were in mid Air Like iff it was proforming A Wheeley.

As the Tractor kept crassing Cotton Rolls on its back Tires, and me I'm with the Tractor's gear shift stuched deep inside my Stomach. The Tractor would Sway From side to side, At the same time the Gear Shift was Zig Zaging inside of me. As the Tractor's Gear Shift continued on Zig Zaging deep inside my body

I knew I had to stop the Tractor, cause iff it kept moving I would be Toren Apart. There was No doubt in my mind that I had reached the (Point oF No Return) A do or Die situations. I had to reach the wires and Pull them apart to kill the Tractor's engine or be Killed myself, iF the Tractor would continue on moving.

But to reach Forwards, That would mean to push against the Tractor's Gear Shift, That was already deep inside of me. I knew that my Bladder was gone cause I could smell the stink of my urines the Tractors Gear Shift had Trespassed it I had weted my Pants. I also could sense that my left Leg was already Paralized I couldn't move it. As the Tractor kept moving I kept thinking was I going to

Let this steal monster drag me all over this
Field and let its Gear Shift tare me to Pieces.

As I had push againest the Gear Shift I Felt it
going deeper into my Stomach. The Pain was
unbearable, I could see that I needed at leaste
two more inches to be able to reach the wires.

I glance toward my stomach I could see most
of the Tractor's Gear Shift was already inside
my Stomach. That instant I had Felt the
Tractor was crossing another cotton Roll the
Tractor started to sway again at the same time
the Gear Shift begun to Zig Zag inside of me.

But as luck would have it, when the Tractor's
Gear Shift was Zig Zaging deep inside of me
it had pushed me toward those wires. When I
had Felt my Finger's touching the wire's, I made
a Fist grabing the wires, and I pulled with
all my might I heard the wires sparking
when they come Apart, Killing the engine
right Away. I had remained Pired between the
Stirring wheel, and The Iron Box that was
welted on the Trailer's Hitch.

As I had mantion beFore, my blood started
gushing out of my wound cause of that bumpy
dirt roads. I had to press my Fingers and Thumb
together and push them deep inside my wound
to prevent the blood From Gashing out of the wound.
It worked some what, but every now and then
I could see some of my Blood Squirting out in
between my Fingers and my Thumb.

Finally we had come onto the Farm Road
as soon that we hit that Farm Road I could Feel
the Pick-up going Faster and Faster.

Within seconds the Truck was going as Fast as it could, I remember Thinking that Although

We were going A Hundred Miles per Hour there was No doubt Whatsoever in my mind that my Death was catching up to me.

Please, Please don't close your eyes the men in Black kept insisting as I layed on his Laps as the Four Tires of the Pickup Kept Roaring beneath us on the way to the Hospital. Because of my lost of Blood I musta been going In and Out of my Conscious, I couldn't Keep my eyes open as hard as I was trying.

That Beautiful Sleepy Sensation kept getting Stronger, that I kept closing my eyes, I just wanted to go to sleep. But the man in Black kept Shaking me so I would wake up. The Fright Look in his eyes, and him begging Please, Please keep your eyes open, Had convinced me that I was to Die at any Second Now laying on a Total Stranger's Lapes, The man that wore Black. When Suddenly I had heard what For a Second I thought somebody was crying. I had asked the man in Black, What's that sound he look behind and said (El Transito) meaning (The Hiway Patrol) By then the Sirens were Loud and Clear, as he over took us, The voice on the Loud Speaker said alright Follow us as we sped toward the Hospital.

The Loud Sirens was keeping me awake, I was Looking at the man in Black's Hat as he kept shading my Face with it. As I kept glancing to the side of the Hat into the Far Sky, what Happen Next has to be the most Beautiful thing that could ever happen to a Dying Son.

9

As the man in Black—^kept^ Shading my Face From the
Sun with his hat, as I was Looking into the Far Sky

There it was, A big Glowing Ball of immense
Alumination. I was stuned as I saw that it was
coming down straignt at us.

I kept watching the Big Glowing Ball coming
at us, I still remember asking myself is this
Big Glowing Ball, is it in Heaven, Am I death?
I musta been unconscious or Delirious because
what had happened next it still stuns me
every time I think of my awful accident.
I couldn't Blink an eye as I kept staring at the big
Glowing Ball, that I was sure it was coming at us.
The Glowing of the Big Ball was Fading
away Now, as it was getting Closer to the Speeding
Truck as I was being rush to the Hospital.
To my Amazement as the Glowing of the Big Ball
kept Fading away an image of a Woman was
Forming. Like a Divine Angel descending
From The Heavens, The Dwellings of our Lord.
I could clearly see her out stretch arms to her
Sides, she was waring a most Beautiful Gowd
getting closer to us. By now the Angel Woman
Was very close to the speeding Truck, I kept
Looking at her Beautiful Gown, For a Second I
Thought The Angel was smiling at me.
I kept staring at her Beautiful smile on
her Divine Face, Suddenly, My Loving Heart was
(Thunder Bolt Stricken) The same instant I had
Recognized the Face of the Smiling Angel.
Oh my God, Oh my God, is you, (is you Mother)
you came, you came (Mother you came.)

There was no doubt in my mind that it was
My Saint Mother as I kept watching her

descending From the Sky, Soaring through Air in
Her Amazing Grace. She made a perfect Landing
in the back oF the Speeding Truck, She cubed Her
adoring, Tender, Gentle, hands caressing my Bloody
Face, Saying to me, (Todo Estara Bien, Hijo Mio)
Meaning (Everthing will be Fine, My Son)
    Her caressing Loving hands had convinced
me that my Saint Mother had come to me, At my
most Desperate Times oF Need.
        So this was how I was to Die, with my
Saint Mother's Gentle hands cubed caressing
Her dying Son's Face. God had answered my Deep
Silent Prayer, when I had asked him to let me Live
So I could see my Saint Mother, even iF it was
going to be For the Last Time. Call me Stupid,
ignorant or A complede Fool. But till this very
day I Trully believe that my Saint Mother rode
with me on the Back oF that Speeding Truck,
As I was mortally wounded, and was being Rush
to the Hospital.
        And to realize that my Saint Mother was
Two Thousand Mile's Away, yes God had
(Heaven Sent) my Saint Mother to me, Not in
Person, But in her Divine Spirit. Her Gentle
Touches as she was caressing my Bloody Face
Saying to me (Todo Estara Bien, Hijo Mio)
(Everthing will be Fine, My Son.)
        Her wonderFul words oF Comford had
given me the Strength, and will power to Live.

"

The Immense Love was the main reason I had
servived that awful accident. (The immense love)

   Love of a Son For his Saint Mother, and the love
of a Saint Mother For Sony Me.
       And a good thing I had servived, cause a Few years
latter I met the girl of my Dream's and of my
heart's Desire's. That became the wonderful,
Beautiful, caring, and loving Mother of our
Four Handsome Son's.
               For what is love?
Love to me has to be The most wonderful and
The most Beautiful Sensation that still's stands
in ones heart when all else is either Death or Gone.
(Death) like my Golden Couple my Loving Parents.
(Gone) like the Girl of my Dearms and of my Heart
Desires Zulema, God bless her Loving Heart.
       I will Forever be thankful to Her For Looking
my way, me a mire Cripple, I could Hardly Walke.
Oh my God, She had said Yes to me asking Her to be
my Sweetheart. From that wonderful moment
on I knew that She had been (Heaven Sent) to me
by our Lord. Again I could Hardly Walk, with
Her kind loving way's toward me, she would
always maded me Felt Like She was carrying me
every time we would go from one place to
Another. That she would always remained me of
   (Foot Prints in the Sand)
The Immense Love that was, but unfortunate it
came Apart, But For me it still Prolonges On and on
And on. One doe's the best that one can with
the immense love toward that very special
Individual, Many a times one's Best in Not enough
which is most unfortunate Because it Has to do.

In a true sense, IF I may compare myself to the Prospector's of the passed I'am the

Most Fortunate of them all, Hand's down.

It's a well Known Fact of the (Gold Rush) in The United States of America. In year 1849, In the state of California to be more Precise. People From many Nations Left their Loves ones behind to Prospect For that Elusive treasure (Gold), they became Known as (The Forty Niner's) only a Few Found Gold.

But For me, My Gold came in more Beautiful Form's. In the 1940's I was being raised by my Golden Couple in the Form of my Loving Parent's. In the 1960's I met The Girl of my Dream's and of my Heart Desires, The Girl with a Golden Heart, In the Form of Zulema. As my Beautiful wife she became my Precious Gold mine, Producing Four Golden Nuggets

In the Form of our Four Handsome Son's.

And Last but not Leaste came my most Precious Golden Dust, In the most Beautiful Form, my Beautiful Grand Children. Although it's been many many year's that my togetherness in merroge with the Girl with the Golden Heart came Apart. When the Thought's of her crosses my mind, I can still sense that my Loving Heart, Still Weep's For Her.

Ain't that Amazing? Yes indeed it is, and most wonderful too. Because of That Girl, in my Loving Heart are 8 Beautiful Girls my Grand dauther's, That I have Loved Immensely and For Ever, yes indeed (Pure Golden Dust.)

B

Also 4 Handsome Grandson's, more Pure Gold.
There it is that wonderful Number, 4 Golden Dust.

Just like our 4 Golden Nuggat's. In my Final
Analyses I am most Lucky and very Fortunate
that my Beautiful GrandChildren came into my
Loving Heart For me to Love Immensely and
Forever, Because if they Hadn't come into my
Heart to Loved

I would've Felt, Like an Ocean without it's
Water, Like the Moon without it's Shine, Like the
Nights without it's Star's, Like the Forest
without it's Trees, Like the Desert without
it's Sand. But since They are in my Loving
Heart to Love Immensely and Forever. Rest assure
that every time Grand PaPa Chapa, See's The Ocean
The Moon, The Stars, The Forrest or The Desert.

They will be a constant remainder of my
Most Precious (Golden Dust.) my most Beautiful
(Treasure) my GrandChildren.
In a true Sense They will Forever be (The Love
of my Love's) or in Spanish, Siempre Seran
(El Amor De Mis Amores.)

A Few day's after my surgury two Young Doctors
came into my Hospital's room. I had told them that I
was in a lot of Pain, They said you will get a
Pain Shot every 4 Hour's. Then I arked them how long
will it take For my Left Foot to get better.

One of the Doctor's said Look young Man
you are very Lucky to be alife. The Tractor did
a lot of Damage inside your stomach The Gear
shiEt Pursture part of your Guts went
through your Bladder, tore ligaments, mucles,
and Nerve's, I am afraid your Foot is Paralized.

You mean I'll be a Cripple I said, No you won't
become a Cripple he said, We don't think you

Will ever walk again, you are Destined to a
Wheel Chair. I Felt that I wanted to Puke
I Felt Nauseated at the thought that I was to
Spend the rest of my Living days on a Wheel Chair.
The Doctor's kept Looking at me as I lyied
on that Hospital's bed in a lot of Pain, the only
only thing I could sense in their Staring eye's
was not concern, Those eye's only had Pity on me.
That instant I knew that my Death would be a
Blessing, Then to become a Pathetic, Pityful
Sight of a Human Bean, I knew that I
Wanted no part of that Life.
For month's I kept begging, imploring to God to
take me away, I couldn't stand the excruciating
Pain Not even For 4 Hour's. I had layed on my
Death bed For Nine Month's, I had been
Withering Away From 160 Pound's to 88 Pound's.
I Looked Pathetic at 88 Pound's, I had seen Movie's
of war with Adolf Hitler. I was Devastated
Realizing that I Looked exactly like the
Prisoner's of (The Holocaust) of Hitlers
Consentration Camp's, But that was Hitler's
war in the passed. My war (Per Say) was
against God, he hadn't Listen to my begging
imploring to take me Away. Every time the
affect's of my pain shot's would ware off
and I would awake.
I would start cursing God Asking him what
kind of God are you? With tear's of excruciating
Pain I would shout to him I hate you For
Doing this to me. I had the Notion that if I

Would Continue on cursing Him he would
strict Strike me Death and probably Sent me

Straight to Hell. But even iF God would've
Sent me there, that would've been a Blessing
For me. Even iF I would've Burn in the Ever
lasting Flames oF Satten's Own Hell.
    A lot Better. Then to be an Invalient the
Pity oF all the People that would have the
Kindness to Look my Way. Since I had arrived
Mortally would to the little Clinic combination
oF a Hospital, Mary the Nurses Aid had Adopted
me, always calling me my Little Brother.
In a Few Day's Mary's Mother had came to visit
me, Bringing me A Big Wooded CruciFix that
    She Hung on my beds Head Board, the one
that I started cursing a couple oF week's later
She had asked me are you Catholic I said yes, that
I was, and she said so are we. Then to my delight-
ment she said my Name is Paula, just like my
Saint Mother's name. Although they Mexican's
they both Spoke very Poor Spanish so they spoke
English to me. Mary was Dark skin same as
her Mother Paula, But both oF them possessed
WonderFul Loving Hearts, toward me.
    Many a time's especially on Sunday's Mary's
oFF day, when I would wake up, There they
Both were kneeling with their head's Bowed
in silent prayer besides my Bed.
By that time my Faith in God was Gone I was
totally convince that my Prayer's toward Him
would be a waste oF Time. But I wouldn't
Dare tell Mary's Mother Paula, For Fear oF
Insulting Her deep Religion.

It was Sunday Morning when Mary
and her Fiance had walked into my Hospital
Room with a basket Full with Food. Hi Little
Brother, we got permission From The Head Nurse
to take you out on back yard of the Hospital
For A Picnic, with a big Smile on Her Face.
I could see that Mary was very Happy For
me, cause she knew this was going to be my
First time, I was going to be off my bed in
More than Nine Months. Mary Kept saying
come on Push off the bed Little Brother. Joe
Mary's Fiance Finally realized how weak
I was, so He grab me From under my under
arm's and pulled me off the bed like I was
a little child.
Mary Knowing my left Foot was still in a
Lot of Pain that not even my bed Sheet's
could touch it. Because it would Feel like I
still had the Tractor on Top of it.
That's why Mary had grabed me From my knees
and they had Transfered me onto The Wheel Chair.
Mary's Fiance proceeded to Pick up the Basket
Full with Food and headed toward the door.
Mary was rounding the Wheel Chair's Back, to
start pushing. When Suddenly I Felt I was
Falling to my right side of the wheel chair's
Rest arm, my Head hit the Railing of my Bed.
I couldn't Hold a sitting position, Mary had
reached and had Pulled me and Held me in A
Sitting position again. At the mean time my
Head was Bobbing side to side and going
Fowards and Backwards I was weaker than
A Newly Born Baby.

Mary shouted a Joe, get me three Pillow's
From the closit and A strap. Mary had put

Pillows all around me, to my Left to my Right
in between the Wheel Chair Arm Rests, Also one
on my Back. As she is straping my Chest to
The back of the wheel Chair to keep me on A
Sitting position. I could see that Her eye's were
Very sad. Because she had Probably realized
that She and her Fiance had just Lifted A
Life Corpse off of that Hospitals Bed, Me
her Little Adopeted Brother. Although I was
Straped to the Wheel Chair on a Sitting position
I wasn't able to Hold on. So I let my weak
body Lean to my right and I layed my Bobbin
Head on the Pillow.
As Mary is pushing me through the Hall way
I had Notice the Hall wall's had been covered
with Smoked Mirror glass, but one could still
detect one's Image. When Mary had stop to
open the door leading to the back yard.
I had glance toward the Wall Mirror, The
Appalling, Disgusting, Pity Ful, sight of Pure
Human Waste had Dismayed Me to the
most absolute and Far, Far Beyond the most
Extreme, That I was in Total Disbelief that
It was Me on the Reflection of that Mirror.
We had Finally made it to the back yard, it
had a Big Table under a Nice shadey Tree.
The morning Breeze had Filled my lungs
With Fresh Air, it Felt very Good. Almost
10 months without Fresh, and Now here I was
outdoors, But I was very weak and my Pain was
coming back, Mary had cut up an Enchilada

For me that her Mother cooked and had sent some For our Picnic.

Mary had set me on a sitting position so she could Feed me, but my Head kept kept Bobbin side ways and Forwards and Backwards, that I kept Knocking The pieces of Enchilada off Mary's Fork. She said Little Brother I'll Feed you when you are laying in bed, she was
Having Problems with her Speech, like IF she wanted to cry. I said it's alright Sis I am not Hungry, would you tell that Nurse to give me my Pain shots Every Time I would say Sis, to Mary her Face would Lit up with Happieness, but Not that time.
I had layed my Bobbin head Back on the Pillow, The Nurse came with my Pain Shots I had asked them to move me under Another tree Away From their Table. The affect's of The Pain shot were making me Sleepy, but I could Hear Mary's Sobbing whispering to Joe saying look at my Little Brother They are Killing Him in this Hospital. Her sad Glances Toward me were of deep Concern (not Pity) Concern Like A True Loving Sister.
By the time I knew it Mary and her Fiance are putting me back on my Bed. I musta dozed off with the pain shot I was given at the Yard.
Joe said to Mary I will be back to pick you up, I have an errand to do. I'll stay here with my Little Brother and wait For you. Mary had comb my hair and creamed my Face, Then she had asked me can I do anything else For you I said Yes, Can you bring me A Gun.

The awFul ReFlection oF me on that Mirror kept coming to my mind that I was

Determine that I didn't wanted to see it Again (Not ever) And the only way ~~was~~ to be Certain was with a Gun, Looking Like that I had No Reson to Continue on being Part oF the Human Race. years beFore I had told my Saint Mother that I was going to bring Home A BeautiFul Girl to be Her dauther in law My Saint Mother Bless her Loving Heart had Said as long as she is A good wiFe to you, Looks are not important. I had said it's important to me, cause she would give me BeautiFul Children, Just Like Her.

God had make me a Bundle oF weak Bones with a No good Limb, and at 88 Pound's I Looked like an Ugly Monster. No girl in Her right mind would've Looked my way, Much Less have Romantic Feeling toward me. Since God had reFused to take me away I had to terminate it on my own.

My Golden Couple my Loving Parent's And most oF my Loving Siblings Had Come and Gone They were Following the Cotton Harvest. I had been (A Milero,) I had become the Fastest cotton-o F most oF Them and had been very proud oF it. And now I couldn't Pick my very weak and very Skinny Body oFF my Bed. (Only The Strong Survive's) And since my Saint Mother was strong, I knew She would get over my Death. Besides I was Certain that it would be Best For all concernd. For I knew that For Strong Bodys, LiFe goes On.

20

And I was very very weak.
Beside's it was Going to be Like Our Golden
Couple our Loving Parents, use to tell us
all their Loving Children.

Death will separate us For A while
The Lord Would Reunited us For Eternity.

I have decided to start writing Again
I hope and pray y'all are able to read
my Awful writing and my Grammar.
I only use commas and Periods and most of
the Times They are at the wrong Places.

Keep in mind I am only A Fifth Grader.
Beside's who did y'all exspected (Shit Spear)
I Beg Y'all's Pardon, I meant (Shake Spear) Ha Ha.

$\mathbf{45}$

CHAPTER

The Accident

I had never worked in a cotton gin before, but Ruben had found a job at a gin, so I planned to work with him for a few weeks to keep him company. I was a little skeptical, but I was up for a new challenge. The idea of working there was better than the thought of working in the fields.

The cotton season was over, so work in the gin started. The gin was very big. Big doors allowed tractors to pull trailers full of cotton inside, where big overhead tubes would suck the cotton out of the trailers and into the gin, which would blow it to machines that would separate the cotton from the seeds. The cotton was put into big bales that weighed as much as five hundred pounds.

After I had worked about a week, I was doing well. It was hard work, but I liked it. I missed my family and being outdoors, but the gin was my work. One worker would hook up trailers filled with cotton to tractors and pull them in and underneath the vacuum tube while another worker would climb up the trailer and direct the vacuum tube.

One day, I pulled a trailer of cotton that weighed over five thousand pounds, got out, and pulled the pin out between the tractor and the trailer to unhook it. I got back on the tractor and drove forward. I saw that the trailer was still following the tractor. I put the tractor in neutral, climbed down, and kicked where I had taken the pin out. I got in the tractor and drove off, but the trailer was still following me. I got down again, but instead of going around to the pin, I made a big mistake. I stood facing the wheel with my left hand holding the clutch. I shifted from neutral to first gear as my left hand was keeping the clutch in. I struck the coupling between the tractor and the trailer with the pin I had pulled out to break it loose, but my left hand slipped from the clutch and the tractor moved forward. I fell, and one wheel of the tractor pinned my right leg. I could feel the weight. I could do nothing. The wheel was rolling over my leg and slowly heading for my groin and chest as it was still dragging the trailer. I thought I was dead. The wheel rolled over my chest and was coming straight at my head.

I saw Mike, the other worker on the trailer, open their eyes wide. I thought, *They look funny*, and I laughed. I turned my head at the last minute, and the wheel grazed the side of my head and rolled over my shoulder. It was just a matter of seconds, but it felt like eternity. I tried to push the wheel off me, but it was way too heavy. I did not know how I survived its weight. I was in shock, but I realized I was alive and in little pain. Mike yelled to the other workers, and they came running as did Ruben. I stood up and said I was okay, but then, my body just gave out. I fell to the ground. My brother picked me up. "Are you hurt?" he asked. I said, "My right leg hurts, but I don't think it's broken."

The manager of the gin drove me to the hospital. On the way, he asked me if I felt all right. I said, "Yes, I feel fine." He asked, "Well, do you still want to go to the hospital?" I said, "I guess not." I thought, *Man, you were lucky*. He turned around and drove back to the gin. Ruben encouraged me to get some X-rays. "No, I'm okay," I said. He said, "Let's go back to the house. Tomorrow, we're going back home to Edinburg."

I was very happy with that. It had been a long season, and I could not wait to get back and see all my friends and family. That night, Mike and another worker at the gin came over to say goodbye; they bought some beer with them. Mike looked at me and said, "Man, I couldn't believe it when I saw the tractor going over you. You were very lucky the trailer stopped moving. If that had rolled over you, you'd be dead."

I said, "Mike, you saved my life."

He said, "But I did nothing to help you!"

I said, "Mike, when I saw your eyes get so big and almost coming out of your sockets, I laughed, and by laughing, my chest expanded right as the wheel was rolling over it. That saved me."

I told Mike not to tell my brother I was hurting all over. I did not want to go to the hospital. The tire left marks on my chest and scraped part of the left side of my face. "What happened today was miraculous," I said. "That wheel was so heavy that I felt I was about to explode, and then it was over."

Mike and his friend left, and my brother and I talked for a while before going to bed. I could not sleep, however, due to the pain. As I lay there crying for most of the night in pain and doubting myself, I tried to understand why I was still alive. I knew that was not the end of my life.

46

CHAPTER

Walking Away from the Fields

Yes, no more pulling cotton, but this was not the end of my life; that was just a short chapter in my life, and the rest was coming. In the cotton fields, I had been great. My achievements were something to be proud of, but only another milero would understand that. I was one of the last to achieve that honor. Mileros performed feats that took astounding will, amazing strength, and much pride that kept them pushing on. But I knew the days of the mileros were coming to an end and would become history. The fire within me would disappear. I would never again reach my marker and feel the thrill of doing so. But my family and I were escaping that prison.

Some of my brothers and sisters had left the cotton fields, and I was at a crossroads wondering if I could make it in another world in as fulfilling a way. What a life I had lived. What a way of making a living—traveling and working. My life so far had been mostly highs but some lows too in the fields, and I wondered if I could live without that. I had become very skilled in twenty different kinds of field work, but those skills were becoming worthless.

People were tired of all the traveling and their children missing so much school. There were other jobs at that time, so finding workers was harder, and the cotton machines were taking over.

The Vietnam war caused the end of picking for many Mexican families as their young men enlisted or were drafted and did not take over their parents' roles in the fields. I knew my number would be called. Three of my brothers had served in the military, but I would be the only one to serve during wartime. I would be the last in my family to serve, and the last in my family to become a milero. My fate was waiting for me.

Ruben and I drove home to Edinburg, a place I loved. Main Street included stores, the courthouse, movie theaters, pool halls, and drive-ins. The street was only about six blocks away, so we would walk to town on Saturdays and Sundays to eat, meet friends, and have fun. All my friends lived there. It was always great to go back to Edinburg; it was something special. This was the end. No more going on those trips. That part of my life was over, but it would stick with me forever. I had sacrificed so much for that way of life, but it had taught me to push on, become confident, trust myself, and not fear the world. This lazy, good-for-nothing, Mexican cotton picker was going to war to prove himself again.

47 CHAPTER

My War

"Pictures from Vietnam ~ circa 1967. Serving the orphans on Thanksgiving. Martin is pictured on the top left corner."

"Hanging out with my army buddies."

"My best friend Lupe Trevino in Vietnam 1969."

After two months in Edinburg, I found a job working in grocery store. Then my brother Roman, who was living in New York City, called and asked me if I wanted to work at Pancho Villa's, a Mexican restaurant in New York in which he was part owner. I said yes, and he sent me a plane ticket. It arrived the same day as did a letter from Uncle Sam. My trip to New York would be delayed for two years, but Uncle Sam would take care of me, and at last, this milero would see war.

We were leaving our country where in many states we were disliked, and many were being sent to another country, Vietnam, where we were hated too not because we were Mexicans but because we were Americans who were fighting them. I thought that if we made it back, things would change for us and we would be welcomed as Americans. Maybe I was asking for the impossible, but I knew one way or another, I would go there. The army became my home, my family.

Apollonio, little brother, you and the cotton fields will always be a big part of my remarkable and unbelievable past. Little brother, we shared only little time together in this world. Maybe in the other world, we will be able to play together again, and maybe there will be cotton fields to pick too. I have never forgotten you and never will. You will always be my little angel. In some of my dreams and thoughts, you were there, little brother, and those memories will forever be inside me. Your baby face is forever implanted in my mind, and I know you will never get old.

I am thinking of you, little brother as I am flying to Vietnam perhaps because I feel closer to heaven and thus closer to you. And, little brother, now you know my story and our family's history. I must go now. I will carry you within me always. Pray for me, my little brother, my little angel.

The captain of the plane announced, "If you look to your right, you'll see Vietnam." I was sitting by a window, and I saw only lights over some parts of the country and tracer rounds being fired from helicopters. Some fighting was going on. We saw only the tracer rounds, not the helicopters. We were amazed. The plane became quiet. We were all apprehensive, fearful, concerned. We were in Vietnam at last. I looked at other soldiers trying to gain some strength, support, and emotional toughness. None of us wanted to fail our families, our heritages, or ourselves as we faced the unknown. We wondered if we would return and see our families again. The plane landed. We were rushed to green buses with painted windows through the heat and humidity on the other side of the world.

The bus driver told us to relax because we were in a safe area. I thought, *Relax? I'm in Vietnam!* He said, "I'm taking you to a camp. You'll be there for some days until you're processed and sent to your units." I could not sleep. I felt insecure, and I feared the unknown. In my mind, the enemy was everywhere. I never prayed so hard in my life in Spanish and in English. I kept reminding myself, *You didn't have to be here. You volunteered to be send here, you dummy. Javier told you never to volunteer for anything.*

I had hometown friends who were in Vietnam. I felt I had to go. It was not that I wanted to be a hero; I just believed it was my war too. This cotton picker was in Vietnam, away from the comforts of home, far from the cotton fields on the other side of the world and facing a strange enemy hoping to prove himself worthy of serving his country.

"Taken at Martín's parents' 50th wedding anniversary
~ His parents and his siblings. circa 1978."

"Painting of Martín's parents: Martíniano and Paulina."

"Martín's sisters: top row ~ Odilia, Olga, Otilia;
bottom row ~ Olivia, Menerva"

"A copy of Pancho Villa's Menu."

Pancho Villa's Restaurant

Established in New York City in 1965 at 78th Street and Second Avenue by our families brother Roman Chapa *(1936-1995)*. Roman's dream was to create an authentic Mexican Restaurant, complete with historical flavor and Mexican culture, on the East Coast. To expand upon and both complement his brother's dream, Martiniano Chapa selected to establish second in a series of Pancho Villa's Restaurants. Pancho Villa's will always serve you the best Mexican food and cocktails. Thus fulfilling Roman's dream and legacy. *A Family—Run, Quality Mexican Restaurant.*

Pancho Villa's Restaurant offers a "Revolutionary" blend of Mexican Culture and fabulous food. Mexico's colorful history comes alive with such images that depict scenes from the Mexican Revolution. Pancho Villa, the most universally known participant in the Revolution, has became a romantic figure to people all over the world.

Authentically prepared Mexican cuisine is the speciality of Pancho Villa's Restaurant. The extensive menu includes tasty Appetizers, Mexican Combinations, Chicken Specials, Mariscos and Our Famous Sizzling Fajitas. Offered for your enjoyment large variety of Tropical Drinks and Mexican Beers. **Your host the Chapa family**

"Zoomed in story of our Pancho Villa's Restaurants."

148

Huntington, L.I. Larchmont, N.Y.

Asbury Park, N.J. New York City

"Restaurants that were owned by family members and myself."

with 4 Brothers at 'ancho Villa's

Texas Rio Grande brothers' parents U. S. when the 'e young. The all now U. S. they still know aside and out. lew York, a bast e who are fond of and there are s of it. There is -Mexican, the n, and hardest of ry special kind. iny, called Tex- lla's specializes ,although true can be found

hful patrons is sa, born a n in San An- lirector of the ge and Culture arbosa claims io Villa's is as x cooking as York. eem to agree, its year-round ind authentic seems to be ings. nosphere are rists who are ngs (except

Favorite dishes on the menu are the classic Guacamole sa..! made from mashed Avacad.. from young tender cactus (thorns removed of course); combination plates of Tacos and Enchiladas and so on.

Then there are the popular Mole (say"mol-a") dishes and the typical Mexican deserts, Flan and Mango with ice cream.

Sangria, topped with Brandy comes in fruited pitchers and

there's a wide selection of Tequil. cocktails. "Cuidado" as the Mexicans say - "careful".

If you don't know Mexican food would like to try, Pancho Vill..is a great place to star and the Brothers Chapa will guide you into the delights of that unique cuisine.

Craig Claiborne, formerly o' The New York Times gave th restaurant two stars. Some people think he stopped two stars short.

THE BROTHERS CHAPA – (l to r) Israel, Javier, Martin Roman all of whom, with typical Latin grace and charm, pre over the goings on at Pancho Villa's, a favorite restaurant w ficianados of Mexican food.

"My brothers and I in our restaurant days ~ Early 1970's.
Clipping from a news article about us. Pictured left to right:
Israel, Javier, Martíniano, & Roman. Not pictured: Benito."

"My grandfather, Apolonio Ybarra."

Printed in the United States
by Baker & Taylor Publisher Services